Using Picture Books to Teach Writing With the Traits

An Annotated Bibliography of More Than 150 Mentor Texts With Teacher-Tested Lessons

**RUTH CULHAM &
RAYMOND COUTU**

K–2

■SCHOLASTIC

New York • Toronto • London • Auckland • Sydney
Mexico City • New Delhi • Hong Kong • Buenos Aires

To Terry Cooper, whose compassion, conviction, and wisdom nourish us daily

Editor: Raymond Coutu
Cover design by Maria Lilja
Interior design by Holly Grundon
Photos by Tim Findlay
Copy Editor: Shelley Griffin

ISBN-13: 978-0-545-02511-9
ISBN-10: 0-545-02511-7
Copyright © 2008 by Ruth Culham.

All rights reserved. Published by Scholastic Inc.
Printed in the U.S.A.
4 5 6 7 8 9 10 23 12 11 10 09 08

Contents

Introduction

> "We need to consider picture books
> as literature—not children's
> literature—but as *literature*."
> —*Thomas Newkirk*

Picture books are a visual delight for readers of all ages for many reasons. Maybe it's the illustrator's use of colors or materials, which can transport the reader to the writer's world. The art alone can entice the reader to return to the book again and again. Or maybe it's the designer's use of fonts or his clever layout. Maybe it's the writer's elegant prose that beckons the reader back for a second or third reading. Most likely, however, it is the combination of all three—illustrations, design, and words—working together to create a magical experience for the reader.

The more than 150 books we share with you in *Using Picture Books to Teach Writing With the Traits: K–2* are beautifully illustrated, designed, and written. These are books we return to again and again for our own enjoyment and to share with teachers of young readers and writers. It's an eclectic collection, containing favorite titles you'll recognize, which are essential to any picture book bibliography, and many brand-new titles by authors who deserve to be heard and celebrated.

There is great teaching potential in picture books. We can use them to model the writer's craft. By analyzing the text through the lens of one or more of the traits of writing—ideas, organization, voice, word choice, sentence fluency, conventions, and presentation—students see firsthand how writing works. They see how all the pieces of the writing puzzle fit together to make stories and informational text clear and enjoyable. The thoughtful understanding of craft is our primary reason for sharing these books with you.

To get you started, we include 18 step-by-step lesson plans, based on books included in the bibliography. These lessons focus on key qualities of each trait and lead students to writing with the traits clearly in mind. Using the picture books as mentor texts allows you and your students to read and examine text from the perspective of the writer. So, while we encourage you to read and enjoy these books with your students, we also hope you'll employ the ready-to-use lesson plans to develop specific student writing skills in each of the traits.

We suggest you read this book for two purposes:

1. **Enjoyment.** We'd like you to begin by reading the annotations with the sole purpose of getting to know the books. Jot down your favorites and think about getting copies at your bookstore, at your library, or online. Whether you are drawn to the realistic, fanciful, or informational, take time to enjoy these fine texts as high-quality literature.

2. **Professional growth.** From there, read the lessons and annotations with an eye toward using them to inform your writing instruction. You may, for example, be interested in lessons that develop writing skills in the voice trait, so you might focus on the books and lessons in that chapter. This is a finely honed collection of mentor narrative and expository texts chosen to help you inspire young writers. The addition of these books to your teaching life will enrich it beyond measure.

It seems fitting, then, to highlight a unique book right up front—a book that shows students how picture books are written, designed, and published. Read this book to students to get right inside the writing process and demonstrate how writers and illustrators create. After you read, talk about the pleasures and challenges of writing strong, original texts, issues most primary students are just beginning to understand.

What Do Authors Do?

Eileen Christelow, Author and Illustrator
Clarion Books, 1995

LESSON FOCUS: THE WRITING PROCESS

In this lesson, students learn, from the author's perspective, how ideas germinate into full-blown stories. Christelow shows clearly where ideas come from, how they are drafted and revised, and how they wind up as books. It's a charming text, intended to teach and entertain at the same time.

MATERIALS:

❋ a copy of *What Do Authors Do?*

❋ cut-apart list described in step #1 below

❋ pencils, pens, markers, crayons

❋ drawing paper

WHAT TO DO:

1. Make an overhead transparency of the following list, cut apart the items, and mix them up.

    ❋ Think of an idea using a favorite book or activity as inspiration. Talk about it with another writer before you write.

    ❋ Write your idea down and add details.

    ❋ Read your draft to another writer. Does he or she have suggestions to make it better?

    ❋ Keep writing. Add pictures.

    ❋ Check the writing for mistakes. Compose a final copy.

    ❋ Share your finished piece with family members and friends.

    ❋ Start planning your next piece.

2. Read *What Do Authors Do?*, showing the pictures as you go.

3. Tell students they are going to capture the steps of the writing process that Christelow describes in her book.

4. Pick up a strip, read it aloud, and ask students to help you decide where it goes. Move each strip to make room for the new one, changing the order as necessary as you go.

5. When you have all the strips in order, read them aloud as a group. Ask students if there are other steps in the writing process that they recall from the book and, if so, where they fit into the list.

6. Make a bulletin board of each item in the list. Put students in pairs and ask them to illustrate one of the steps. Put their drawings next to the appropriate items on the bulletin board to help students remember the steps.

FOLLOW-UP ACTIVITIES:

❋ Ask students which step of the writing process they feel will be the easiest for them and which will be the most challenging. Discuss ways that writers overcome difficulties.

❋ Read and discuss *Ish* by Peter H. Reynolds (see page 48 for a description). Talk to students about how every writer feels "ishy" about what they write, but over time, with lots of help, this feeling turns to confidence.

OTHER PICTURE BOOKS TO INSPIRE WRITING

Aunt Isabel Tells a Good One
Kate Duke, Author and Illustrator
Dutton Children's Books, 1992

This adorable book explains how writers work with character, plot, and setting to tell stories. Penelope, a young mouse, and her Aunt Isabel work out all the elements of a clever story, including the use of details to capture the reader's interest. For example, Aunt Isabel adds villains as she explains to Penelope that stories must have problems to be resolved. This text is a terrific place to begin discussions of what makes a good story as students plan their own pieces.

You Have to Write
Janet S. Wong, Author
Teresa Flavin, Illustrator
Margaret K. McElderry Books, 2002

Stepping into the shoes of the student writer who is told to write but really doesn't want to, Wong shares valuable ideas to get going: The smallest everyday events or observations can make for fascinating reading. An appreciation of the difficulty of learning to write winds through this book. Wong anticipates what will challenge students most and provides the inspiration to find the ideas that will excite those students as writers and, in turn, engage us as readers.

Author: A True Story

Helen Lester, Author and Illustrator

Houghton Mifflin Company, 1997

Lester's autobiography of her writing life is a treasure. She documents her first writing efforts—a grocery shopping list only she could read—to her attempts at writing a picture book and getting it published. Throughout, the reader is reminded that writing is hard, that ideas come from everywhere, and that many runs at the text are necessary to get it just right. Lester's personal journey as a writer is a celebration. Though she is honest about the struggle, she is joyous about the outcome. Students who read this text will get a balanced view of the writing process.

Show, Don't Tell! Secrets of Writing

Josephine Nobisso, Author

Eva Montanari, Illustrator

Gingerbread House, 2004

One of the secrets to good fiction and nonfiction writing is to be descriptive and help the reader fall deeply into the idea. In this visually appealing and interactive book, Nobisso puts the just-right adjective with a noun to make the writing come to life. (Yes, you get to feel textures and push buttons for sounds.) She explores the use of metaphors and similes, too, helping the reader see how images can be created by using all the senses.

CHAPTER 1

Inspiring Ideas

Ideas make up the content of the piece. They are the clear message of the writer coming through to the reader via text and pictures. For primary students to show strength in the ideas trait, we must help them do the following:

❉ find the right topic

❉ select interesting, relevant details

❉ make the content clear through elaboration

Young writers don't always think they have strong ideas for writing. As you read the books in this section together, talk with them about the writer's idea and how often a very simple idea became the inspiration for a whole book. Point out the details as you read. Help students to see that they can use the ideas in these fine books as springboards for ideas in their own pieces.

IDEAS: A DEFINITION FOR PRIMARY STUDENTS

The ideas trait is about the writing's overall message and meaning. It is about the content of the writing. Ideas are strong when they are clear and focused, and move from the general to the specific. Though their texts may not be lengthy, young writers convey ideas by doing the following:

* drawing pictures with bold lines and lots of color

* experimenting with letters and words

* captioning pictures they create themselves and gather from sources

* talking about what happened to them or their characters

* asking questions and making lists about things that interest them

* noticing significance in little things and events

PICTURE BOOKS FOR INSPIRING IDEAS

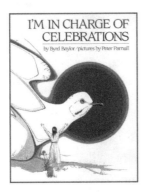

I'm in Charge of Celebrations

Byrd Baylor, Author
Peter Parnall, Illustrator
Scribner's, 1986

This joyous celebration of the earth shows how to find ideas for writing in everyday life. The narrator announces, "Last year I gave myself one hundred and eight celebrations—besides the ones that they close school for." In prose that reads like poetry, she highlights some of her favorite self-proclaimed holidays: Green Cloud Day, Dust Devil Day, and Triple Rainbow Day. Primary writers who fall in love with this book can make lists of their own celebration days as possible topics for writing. See focus lesson, pages 19–20.

Who Is the Beast?

Keith Baker, Author and Illustrator

Harcourt, Inc., 1990

"The beast, the beast! We must fly by! We see his tail swing low and high." So begins this richly illustrated story of the search for an animal hiding in the deep, dark jungle. Is it the tiger whose tail swooshes through several pages? Is it one of the birds hiding in the lush landscape? Your students will be surprised and delighted to find out that beast is actually…them, readers of this delightful book! Baker provides a fine example of how simple details can add up to a big idea.

Fireflies!

Julie Brinckloe, Author and Illustrator

Aladdin Paperbacks, 1985

This magical little piece of writing is sure to delight. Sometimes the smallest moments in a story are what make it special. This book celebrates one of those moments, focusing the reader on the significance of an important life lesson—that sometimes in order to keep something, you have to set it free.

Trouble on the T-Ball Team

Eve Bunting, Author

Irene Trivas, Illustrator

Clarion Books, 1997

Who doesn't love a surprise—especially a reader? Bunting uses a baseball game as the backdrop for this book. Linda has lost something and, from all accounts, it's something important. As the baseball game unfolds, we get little hints of what it is. Finally, as the game ends, we find out what was lost. The timing is perfect, both on the field and for Linda. Giving little hints throughout—using small moments to make big points—Bunting does this beautifully and offers a technique for young writers to try in their own stories.

Whoever You Are

Mem Fox, Author

Leslie Staub, Illustrator

Harcourt Brace, 1997

Fox's timeless book assures us that no matter who we are and where we live, there are people who are just like us. As this idea plays out, in details showing all the ways humans are similar, Fox treats us to poetic rhythms and cadences. At the end, she tells us, "Joys are the same and love is the same. Pain is the same and blood is the same. Smiles are the same and hearts are just the same—wherever they are, wherever you are, wherever we are, all over the world." Read this important book aloud and invite students to talk about the similarities of people in their town and around the world. Ask students to draw pictures of their school, houses, and favorite activities, and caption them. Then find a school in another part of the world (through a reputable international pen pal Web site such as www.epals.com) and send these pictures to students there so they can connect with your students.

Out of the Ocean

Debra Frasier, Author and Illustrator

Harcourt, Inc., 1998

It's those little moments that inspire the best ideas for writing. Here, Frasier takes us into one of those moments, a quiet walk on the beach. She paints a picture in your mind. Her text is so real, so right, that you can smell the salt air and feel the sand between your toes. This work is perfect for showing how to write about small things so they really resonate with the reader.

Roller Coaster

Marla Frazee, Author and Illustrator

Harcourt, Inc., 2003

Take a small moment, blow it up, and relive it from all of its many interesting angles. That's the way this action-packed piece on roller coasters unfolds. Some writers think they have to write about the whole day or every attraction at the amusement park. Not Frazee. She gives us one moment in time on one ride so clearly that we feel we are experiencing it right along with the characters in the story.

Henry Works

D. B. Johnson, Author and Illustrator

Houghton Mifflin Company, 2004

Johnson proves that children are never too young for biographies. In this book, his fourth about the life of 18th-century writer and philosopher Henry David Thoreau, Johnson explores the idea of work—what it means to work, how one's work is perceived by others, and the importance of finding joy in work. We follow Henry on his way to the cabin in the woods where he writes. It seems he's not doing much of anything along the way—watching the weather, clearing a path, delivering strawberry plants to Mrs. Hawthorne's garden, and so forth. But the careful reader will realize that he is doing much more than gathering strawberry plants. He is gathering raw material for his writings on nature, while, at the same time, helping neighbors in need. A poignant story based on a simple, timeless idea.

The Hello, Goodbye Window

Norton Juster, Author

Chris Raschka, Illustrator

Hyperion Books, 2005

This book won the Caldecott medal in 2006 for good reason: It's a delightful story, featuring Chris Raschka's trademark pictures in vibrant, luminescent colors. A little girl regularly visits her grandparents' old house, which has many interesting features, such as a beautiful garden, a comfy bed, and kitchen walls covered in old photographs and shelves holding glass jars "with lots of everything in them." But the girl's favorite feature is the kitchen window. Through the window, she plays peekaboo with her grandparents. She makes funny faces in its reflection. And, before going to bed, she peers upward from the window to wish the stars goodnight. *The Hello, Goodbye Window* is proof that love truly does make a family—and provides powerful inspiration for writing.

Ugly Fish

Kara LaReau, Author

Scott Magoon, Illustrator

Harcourt, Inc., 2006

Ugly Fish is nasty in every way, on the inside and the outside. He is perfectly happy living alone in his tank, swimming through his driftwood tunnel, feeding on his special briny flakes. So when new fish are introduced into the tank, Ugly Fish makes no effort to welcome them. Instead, he eats them. Eventually, though, he learns his lesson . . . and it's not pretty. You can use this book as a starting point to discuss the natural order of life in the animal kingdom, the pros and cons of sharing a living space, or an all-too-common problem in schools today: bullying. Chances are, there's at least one "ugly fish" on your school's playground, right? From there, have students come up with metaphors to describe other troubling issues in the real world and write about them.

Little Blue and Little Yellow

Leo Lionni, Author and Illustrator

Astor-Honor Publishing, Inc., 1959

The best ideas can stand the test of time. First published in 1959, *Little Blue and Little Yellow* is the story of a blue splotch and a yellow splotch that are good, good friends who play together all the time. One day, though, they become separated and search for each other. When they finally reunite, they hug—so hard, in fact, they turn into one green splotch! Their parents don't accept them at first, but do once they realize that they, too, can turn green if they are willing to hug strongly enough. Use this book to show how one idea can contain many layers of meaning—in this case, to show how colors can be combined to create new colors, to show what constitutes true friendship, and to show how breaking down racial barriers can, indeed, make the world a better place.

All the Places to Love

Patricia MacLachlan, Author

Mike Wimmer, Illustrator

HarperCollins, 1994

In this book, the young narrator takes you on a journey to the rural farm where she grew up. Sensory details enrich lovely passages such as "My grandmother loved the river best of all the places to love. *That sound, like a whisper*, she said"; "…gather in pools where trout flashed like jewels in the sunlight"; and "…the birds surrounded us: raucous black grackles, redwings, crows in the dirt that swaggered like pirates." Can't you see those fish and birds? Read this book to students and ask them about their most vivid thoughts of home. Remind them that their writing, too, can create pictures in the reader's mind.

I Spy Extreme Challenger! A Book of Picture Riddles

Jean Marzollo, Author

Walter Wick, Photographer

Scholastic, 2000

The latest in the series of I Spy books really takes the prize. Children and adults will be fascinated by the complex photographs and challenging riddles that make them want to dive in and find the hidden objects. Becoming aware of little details that someone else might not notice is one of the keys to success in writing ideas clearly. Surely having this book and the others in the series will help student writers sharpen their descriptive powers—and have a blast along the way!

Katie's Sunday Afternoon

James Mayhew, Author and Illustrator

Scholastic, 2004

As primary teachers, you know better than anyone that young children have incredible imaginations. So why not help them apply their magical thinking to writing? This book will get them started. It is the tale of Katie, a little girl who visits an art museum, and finds herself, literally, drawn into paintings by Seurat, Signac, and Pissarro. She takes a dip in the river featured in *Bathers at Asnières*. When the water spills out of the frame and fills the museum, she urges subjects in *Sunday Afternoon on the Island of La Grande Jatte* to step off the canvas to come wade with her. And when the museum begins to flood, she boards a boat in *Port of Honfleur*. Throughout her adventure, Katie makes friends— children depicted in the paintings. Mayhew blurs the line between fantasy and reality, creating a story that will mesmerize young writers.

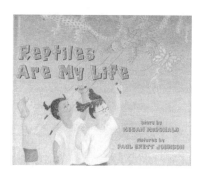

Reptiles Are My Life

Megan McDonald, Author

Paul Brett Johnson, Illustrator

Scholastic, 2001

Books that mix fact and fiction provide good models for writing about factual information in different formats. This text is a great example of just that—a good story combined with all sorts of interesting bits of information about reptiles. It's funny and true to life at the same time—the perfect book to study to learn how to blend genres.

The Perfect Pet

Margie Palatini, Author

Bruce Whatley, Illustrator

HarperCollins, 2003

The pet battle begins! Elizabeth desperately wants a pet, any pet. But there's one little problem: her parents don't. Elizabeth has some tricks up her sleeve to win her parents over, though, including waking them from a dead sleep and begging for a pet. When she finally finds the perfect pet, a bug named Doug, her parents are relieved. Or are they? This upbeat book will inspire kids to write about persuading a parent to get them a pet, or anything else, for that matter.

It's Okay to Be Different

Todd Parr, Author and Illustrator

Little, Brown and Company, 2001

Parr is a 21st-century phenomenon. His wacky characters, high-voltage colors, and themes of peace, love, and understanding have left an indelible mark on children's literature. In this book (1 of 27 as of this writing), Parr explores the ordinary, extraordinary, and sometimes downright silly things that distinguish people from one another—from being bald to being adopted to enjoying macaroni and cheese in the bathtub. By doing so, he sends a message that what separates us is really what unites us. He takes one simple yet profound idea and views it through many lenses, which is something your students can do in their own writing. So read this book to them, encourage them to write, and, in the process, make them feel good for simply being who they are. See focus lesson, pages 21–22.

Worksong

Gary Paulsen, Author

Ruth Wright Paulsen, Illustrator

Harcourt Brace & Co., 1997

Gary Paulsen is best known for his critically acclaimed young adult novels such as *Hatchet* and *The River*, but, as this book proves, he is equally skilled at writing picture books. In spare, lyrical language he looks at what adults do when children are at school and play: work. Thanks largely to the graceful, richly layered oil paintings by Ruth Wright Paulsen, the book is a celebration of the average person—the office worker, the truck driver, the farmer, the nurse, and, indeed, the teacher—whose daily efforts strengthen our economy, uphold our community, and pave the way to a bright future for children everywhere. *Worksong* does not glamorize work. It presents work as the lubricant that keeps our lives running smoothly, the song that defines our days.

The Kissing Hand

Audrey Penn, Author

Ruth E. Harper and Nancy M. Leak, Illustrators

Child Welfare League of America, Inc., 1993

Written in a style reminiscent of classic children's tales, *The Kissing Hand* is about a young raccoon, Chester, who is afraid to leave home for school. His mother calms his fears with one small but powerful gesture: She plants a gentle kiss on the palm of Chester's hand and tells him, "When you feel lonely and need a little loving from home, just press your hand to your cheek and think, 'Mommy loves you….'" From there, Chester trots off to school, confident and happy—but not before planting his own kiss on his mother's palm. Whether a child is transitioning to school, moving to a new home, or dealing with the loss of a loved one, *The Kissing Hand* provides the support and encouragement they need. It proves that picture books not only can entertain, but encourage. It proves that good writing can improve the quality of one's life.

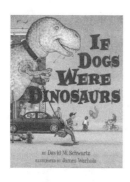

If Dogs Were Dinosaurs

David M. Schwartz, Author

James Warhola, Illustrator

Scholastic, 2005

An effective way to help kids come up with ideas for writing is to ask them "What if" questions: What if you could fly? What if you were elected president of the United States? What if you lived on a farm and rain didn't fall for weeks? Questions like these get kids wondering and writing. Of course, mentor texts help, too—and there isn't a better one than *If Dogs Were Dinosaurs*. Schwartz explores issues of size and scale. Imagine if the moon were as small as a marble, if cruise ships were as small as kayaks, and if molehills were as big as mountains. Life would be very different. Schwartz's way-out wonderings are supported by Warhola's equally way-out drawings, which are sure to bring your students to their knees during read-aloud and have them shouting "Cool!": the highest compliment for any picture book illustrator. See focus lesson, pages 22–23.

Imagine a Day

Sarah L. Thomson, Author

Rob Gonsalves, Illustrator

Atheneum Books for Young Readers, 2005

Imagine a Day is the kind of book that makes children feel that anything is possible. Thomson begins each page spread with the ordinary phrase "Imagine a day…," but follows it up with an extraordinary vision: "…when you forget how to fall," "…when you don't need wings to soar," "…when you build the world around you piece by piece." Gonsalves's breathtaking paintings blur the line between reality and fantasy—between reality and hope, actually. We see people literally construct bridges with their bodies, walk on water, and fly. *Imagine a Day* is an exceptional example of imaginative writing. It provides a good model for students who are interested in tackling that mode on their own. But more important, by sending a message that nothing's impossible, the book gives students the confidence to do it.

Tuesday
David Wiesner, Illustrator
Houghton Mifflin Company, 1991

Some of the best picture books are just that: *picture books*, with no words at all. Take Wiesner's Caldecott-winning *Tuesday*, for example, the story of a pondful of frogs whose lily pads become magic carpets one moonlit night, and they take flight. The frogs drift about the town, past houses, through a laundry line, and even inside one woman's living room. A man reports the incident to the police, but by the time the officers arrive, it's too late; the rising sun has grounded the frogs. *Tuesday* is a visually stunning book. But, with virtually no writing, how can it help children to become better writers? By prompting them to put language to pictures. Wiesner's mesmerizing, magical illustrations draw children in and invite them to tell the story in their own words and, in the process, become better storytellers—and better storytellers become better writers.

The Polar Express
Chris Van Allsburg, Author and Illustrator
Houghton Mifflin Company, 1985

This marvelous tale of magic and imagination is bound to put a twinkle in even the most cynical eye. As the reader moves through the tale of a boy's trip to the North Pole on Christmas Eve, he or she is struck by the words and imagery that create a sense of wonder. The idea behind this book is simple . . . yet never fails to inspire multilayered discussion and writing. See if your students can sum up the theme in just one sentence! Then let them explain.

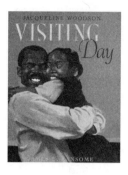

Visiting Day

Jacqueline Woodson, Author

James E. Ransome, Illustrator

Scholastic, 2002

We admire so many things about Woodson: her authentic voice, her carefully chosen words, her plot twists that cut straight to the heart. But mostly we admire her willingness to embrace issues that few writers are willing to, such as substance abuse, racial discrimination, and homophobia. These issues, we know, aren't fit for every classroom. But for children who are touched by them, Woodson's books are a balm. In *Visiting Day*, we follow a little girl as she and her grandmother take their monthly trip to see her father in prison. We see them prepare for the visit, board the bus, and ultimately arrive at the "big old building where…Daddy is doing a little time." We also see the girl's range of emotions: eagerness, sadness, and, ultimately, hopefulness that she and her father will one day share a home again. Like all of Woodson's books, *Visiting Day* does not preach. It is an honest story, inspired by unconditional love.

THREE FOCUS LESSONS ON IDEAS

LESSON 1

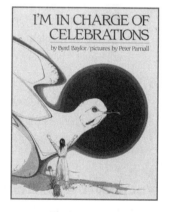

I'm in Charge of Celebrations

Byrd Baylor, Author

Peter Parnall, Illustrator

Scribner's, 1986

TARGET TRAIT: IDEAS

Dust Devil Day, Green Cloud Day, Time of Falling Stars—these special celebrations of the natural beauty of the high Southwest desert are described in such rich detail, the text is almost touchable. As you read Baylor's lines (prose or poetry?), flanked on every page by Parnall's abstract images, it's easy to imagine being right there with the young protagonist as she names each natural phenomenon she observes and creates a special day to commemorate it. Your students can do the same, looking closely at colors, shapes of clouds, and weather patterns in the world around them.

MATERIALS:

❁ a copy of *I'm in Charge of Celebrations*

❁ writing pad or notebook

❁ paper

❁ colored pens, markers, crayons

WHAT TO DO:

1. Read *I'm in Charge of Celebrations* to the class.

2. Ask the students to name their favorite celebrations from the book. Reread descriptions of these celebrations and help students notice that they are inspired by events in life: the shape of clouds, the stars at night, the color of the sky.

3. Take students on a walk outside. As you walk, ask them to write or draw on their pads or notebooks three natural events that are special to them, such as the sound of the wind, the way the sun shines on their faces, the way the air smells when they get away from the school and other buildings.

4. When you return to class, tell them to look at their list from the walk and circle the event they want to write more about and plan a celebration for.

5. When everyone has chosen an idea, give students a piece of 8 ½ x 11 paper, folded into quarters like a book. Tell them that on the front they should draw a picture of the celebration topic and write: "You are invited to a special celebration called _____." On the inside cover, they should explain why this natural event is being celebrated. On the right side of the page, they should write the date, time, and place for their celebration, including whom to contact to respond to the invitation. On the back cover, they may want to draw more pictures.

6. When students have completed their invitations, ask them to talk to a neighbor about why they chose the subject of the celebration. Ask for volunteers to share their invitations with the class. Hang the invitations on a string across a corner of the classroom, along with a cover of the book, so students can read them as time allows.

FOLLOW-UP ACTIVITIES:

❁ Help students plan a class celebration to honor each of the natural events they chose. Have them give a short speech explaining why they made the choice.

❁ Read and enjoy *Everybody Needs a Rock* by Byrd Baylor. Like all Baylor books, this book stresses the importance of uniting with nature. The reader is given ten detailed ways to pick the perfect rock.

LESSON 2

It's Okay to Be Different

Todd Parr, Author and Illustrator
Little, Brown and Company, 2001

TARGET TRAIT: IDEAS

Students notice differences among themselves and other classmates, for better or for worse. But as Parr deftly points out in this book, that which makes us different can also unite. In this lesson, students find pictures and write about what makes each classmate special, interesting, and perhaps different from everyone else. But, when all the drawings are gathered into a special book, they see that those unique qualities are what unites the class; they see a group of wonderful kids with all kinds of talents and interests.

MATERIALS:

❖ a copy of *It's Okay to Be Different*

❖ magazines with many pictures of people, animals, and interesting places

❖ scissors, tape, and glue

❖ paper

WHAT TO DO:

1. Read the book to the class. Discuss the idea behind the book and help students to see the details that Parr uses to make his message clear.

2. Tell students that they are going to make a collage that shows interesting things about themselves. They are to cut out pictures from magazines of favorite pets, places, clothes, hobbies, sports, foods, and other things that represent their interests.

3. Pass out the magazines, scissors, and paper. They should cut carefully, and lay out each picture on the page so it is easy to view. Then give them glue or glue sticks to paste the pictures down.

4. Ask students to label the pictures: "my favorite vacation spot," "my idea of a great dinner," "a sweater that I'd wear in the winter," and so on. Be sure they put their name at the top of the paper.

5. Ask students to go back through the magazines, assign them each a classmate, and have them cut out pictures they think represent that person: a special house, a bus/car, an interesting place, a favorite book, shoes, pictures of people, and so on. Tell them to write on each picture which classmate it represents and give you all the pictures.

6. Paste the pictures to another piece of paper to create a cover for a book that will contain the individual pages that students created. They can help you label the items on the front, just like they did on their own page.

7. As you assemble the book, explain how students are quite different from one another. Bind it or punch holes through the edges at the margin and tie with string. Leave the book out for all to enjoy.

FOLLOW-UP ACTIVITIES:

❊ Share the book with the whole class and identify similarities and differences among students' choices.

❊ Share the book *I Am America* by Charles R. Smith Jr., another fine text that shows how different we can be, one from another, and yet still all be Americans.

LESSON 3

If Dogs Were Dinosaurs

David M. Schwartz, Author
James Warhola, Illustrator
Scholastic, 2005

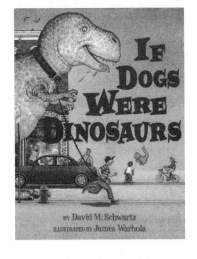

TARGET TRAIT: IDEAS

When students tap into their "fierce wonderings," as writing expert Ralph Fletcher calls them, they ask questions, stretch their imaginations with the answers, and come up with many ideas for topics to write and draw about. In this text, Schwartz asks, "What if?" to help students think about familiar ideas in a new way: What if the moon were a marble? What if germs were as big as gerbils? What if a cruise ship were the size of a kayak? By tapping into the unknown and using clever illustrations to make the idea visible for the reader, Schwartz might inspire students to try their hand at their own size comparisons. Or, they may want to come up with their own "What if" category such as color: What if polar bears were green with purple polka dots? What if the sky were yellow and the sun were blue? What if daffodils were magenta? The possibilities for writing ideas using "What if" as modeled in this text are endless!

MATERIALS:

❊ a copy of *If Dogs Were Dinosaurs*

❊ overhead and markers

❊ drawing paper

❊ pencils, pens, markers, crayons

WHAT TO DO:

1. Read the book to students, stopping to show the pictures as you go. Notice which examples from the book draw the biggest response from students and go back and look at them more closely on a second read.

2. Ask students to tell you what this author's "big idea" is in the book. Discuss with them that he asks the question "What if?" and answers it in a way that shows usual size relationships. Go back to favorite examples to reinforce how this idea comes through in the book.

3. Tell students they are going to write their own "What if?" statements, but they'll use color instead of size in the answer. Using the overhead, show them one or two examples:

   ❊ What if trees were pink and leaves were rainbow striped?

   ❊ What if the ocean were orange and fish had black and white polka dots?

4. Ask students to work in pairs and talk through "What if?" statements of their own.

5. After groups have discussed for a while, ask them to call out their favorite examples and record them on the overhead.

6. Give pairs of students paper, colored markers, and crayons. Ask them to fold their paper into a book by folding it in half, and then in half again.

7. On the front of the book, have them write "What if?"

8. On the inside two pages, have them write out their two favorite examples and illustrate them.

9. On the back of the book, have them write their names and the date.

FOLLOW-UP ACTIVITIES:

❊ Encourage students to think of other ways to show extreme pairs, such as tallest to shortest, widest to thinnest, and heaviest to lightest, as possible ideas for writing.

❊ Share *Biggest, Strongest, Fastest* by Steve Jenkins, which depicts another way to find ideas for writing.

CHAPTER 2

Shaping
Organization

Finding a logical way to present ideas and details is a challenge for all writers, regardless of age. It's easy to provide a formula and have students plug in their text in a pre-programmed manner, but it doesn't make for interesting or effective organization. Instead, students need to discover how text is organized in other books and printed materials and model the organization in their own work accordingly. We can help primary writers develop strength in organization by showing them mentor texts that have the following:

* bold beginnings

* mighty middles

* excellent endings

The picture books in this section are good models of organization. In each, the author has carefully put the details and ideas in a logical order that enhances understanding—the primary goal of organization. By pointing out to students how each of the books is organized, we provide them with excellent examples to try with their own pieces.

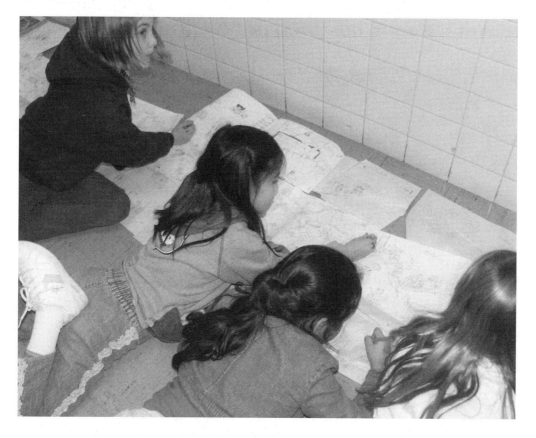

ORGANIZATION: A DEFINITION FOR PRIMARY STUDENTS

Think of organization as the skeleton that holds a building together—the concrete foundation, the steel beams, the weight-bearing timbers. When the building is finished, the skeleton isn't visible. What you see instead are the shapes of the rooms, the finished walls, the windows, the light fixtures. But the building is solid because of its sturdy framework. You know it works. Same goes for writing. If you look closely at the work of even emergent writers, you may see signs of organization, such as:

- several pictures on the same topic, in sequential order
- information grouped by circling, highlighting, and connecting lines
- a clear beginning and/or ending
- use of connecting words such as *and, but,* and *so*
- use of sequencing words such as *first, then, later,* and *the end*
- a sense of time through a sequence of events
- use of labels, titles, and captions
- use of lists

PICTURE BOOKS FOR SHAPING ORGANIZATION

The Magic Fan

Keith Baker, Author and Illustrator

Voyager Books, 1984

Richly illustrated with a detailed Japanese fan, this text is a classic piece that students will want to return to over and over again. Baker's attention to detail and his use of a foldout fan on every page makes the book enjoyable to readers of all ages. You see the clear development of a story, with all of its key elements, and some excellent examples of sequencing and transition words throughout.

I Ain't Gonna Paint No More!

Karen Beaumont, Author

David Catrow, Illustrator

Harcourt, Inc., 2005

In the spirit of David Shannon's classic *No, David!* this book takes on an issue near and dear to most children's hearts: temptation. A young boy discovers a box of paints in a closet and, despite his promise to his mother that he "ain't gonna paint…," he transforms his body, part by part, into a work of art, starting with his head and ending with his feet. Beaumont's bouncy narrative is bound to get your students predicting what will come next with each page turn: "I take some red and I paint my… HEAD!" "I just can't rest till I paint my… CHEST!" "Like an Easter egg, gonna paint my…"—you guessed it—"LEG!" And Catrow's illustrations are nothing short of astounding as he moves from a black-and-white palette at the book's start to a whirlwind of vibrant colors by the end.

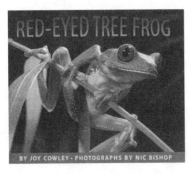

Red-Eyed Tree Frog

Joy Cowley, Author

Nic Bishop, Photographer

Scholastic, 1999

Nonfiction for children has come a long way in the last 25 years. Whereas it used to be made up of dry, voiceless books on a handful of predictable topics, now we have books on the full range of topics of interest to children—from aardvarks to zeppelins—written in a style that is every bit as compelling as good fiction. *Red-Eyed Tree Frog* is a perfect example.

It is the story of a little frog's night-to-morning quest for food in the rain forest, told through Cowley's witty, question-and-answer format and Bishop's stunningly detailed photographs. Children will feel as if they're hopping right along with the frog as he explores the forest, encounters predators, and ultimately makes a meal of a moth. Cowley closes with a detailed "Did You Know?" section, containing fascinating facts that will answer many of the questions this story is sure to raise.

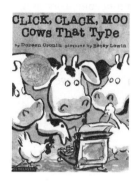

Click, Clack, Moo: Cows That Type

Doreen Cronin, Author

Betsy Lewin, Illustrator

Simon & Schuster, 2000

Stories need problems to be solved. In this uproarious piece, Farmer Brown has a problem, all right. He has cows that type and keep sending him messages about ways to make them more comfortable. It starts with electric blankets and goes on from there. These literate cows turn Farmer Brown's life upside down as a series of letters between the farmer and the cows sets up a back-and-forth organizational structure to move the story forward. Adults will appreciate the subtleties that parallel our working lives.

A Grand Old Tree

Mary Newell DePalma, Author and Illustrator

A. A. Levine Books, 2005

This is the simple story of a tree—a grand old tree that flowered, bore fruit, sowed seeds, and was home to many creatures, from ladybugs to squirrels. Through DePalma's soft, colorful illustrations, we see the tree sprout and shed leaves over many, many years—and ultimately fall when she is old and brittle. Eventually, she decomposes and becomes part of the earth from which she originally grew. The organization of this book couldn't be clearer—in essence, it's a birth-to-death story that students can easily replicate in their own writing. But DePalma teaches them more than a thing or two about writing. They learn from her that all living things, indeed, have a life and, in their own way, sustain life. Therefore, we must honor those things and do everything in our power to protect them.

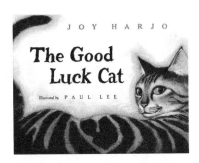

The Good Luck Cat

Joy Harjo, Author

Paul Lee, Illustrator

Harcourt, Inc., 2000

For anyone who has truly loved a pet, this book is for you. The stories are organized to show how Woogie the cat lost each of her nine lives. Tucked between a brilliant introduction and heartwarming conclusion is a story organized around a true idea, not a prescribed number of paragraphs. You will want to use this book for word choice, too. Listen to the beautiful language in the opening paragraph: "I have a cat, a stripedy cat with tickling whiskers and green electric eyes. She has the softest fur in the world. When I pet her she purrs as if she has a drum near her heart." We love this book, and, honest, not because one of Ruth's cats looks exactly like Woogie!

Dear Mr. Blueberry

Simon James, Author and Illustrator

Margaret K. McElderry Books, 1991

This book is organized around a series of letters between Emily, a young girl who thinks she has a whale named Arthur living in her pond, and her teacher, Mr. Blueberry. Mr. Blueberry is understandably skeptical and points out that whales live in salt water and couldn't possibly live in her pond. Unaffected by Mr. Blackberry's response, Emily continues to write to him about Arthur's activities. This enjoyable book shows young writers how letters are organized and may inspire them to start up their own correspondence on a topic of their choice.

City by Numbers

Stephen T. Johnson, Author and Illustrator

Viking, 1998

A perfect companion to Stephen Johnson's other picture book masterpiece, *Alphabet City*, this book challenges us to look closely at our surroundings for numbers. When a writer looks closely to see the details others might miss, we say he or she is working with the ideas trait. That is certainly true for this book, but the way it is organized is worth studying, too. Ask students to find numbers around the school, on the playground, or at home. Then have them bring those numbers back to class and create new texts organized like Johnson's.

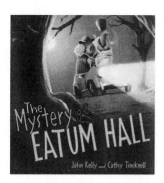

The Mystery of Eatum Hall

John Kelly, Author and Illustrator

Cathy Tincknell, Author

Candlewick Press, 2004

Mysteries are wonderful for teaching about organization because, so often, the organizing device—clues—is what keeps us hanging onto the writer's every word. We can't wait for the next bit of evidence to help us solve the mystery. We reflect, wonder, and anticipate, largely because of the timing of clues. In *The Mystery of Eatum Hall*, Kelly and Tincknell introduce us to the gluttonous Glenda and Horace Pork-Fowler, who have been invited to the country home of Dr. Hunter. They gladly accept because of the lavish meals they'll undoubtedly be served. But when they arrive, Dr. Hunter is nowhere to be found. A diabolical presence is, though. As Glenda and Horace eat their way through the weekend, the reader discovers, through Kelly's ingenious illustrations, that they are being watched. But by whom? And for what reason? This is one delicious mystery!

The Red Book

Barbara Lehman, Illustrator

Houghton Mifflin Company, 2004

A good picture book is the perfect marriage of words and illustrations. But every now and then a book comes along with illustrations that are so expressive and evocative no words are necessary to tell the story. *The Red Book* is one of those books. In it, a young girl from the city finds a book on the sidewalk, while across the world, on a remote island, a boy finds a similar book in the sand. But these are no ordinary books. These books contain magic—magic that eventually unites the two children. There is magic in the storytelling, too. Lehman blends time and space to create a feast for the senses. As Raymond Briggs's *The Snowman* has proven to generations of children, *The Red Book* will prove to your students that illustrations can be every bit as powerful as words in guiding the reader along.

Jake's 100th Day of School

Lester L. Laminack, Author

Judy Love, Illustrator

Peachtree, 2006

Jake has a problem. It's the 100th day of school, and he has forgotten the project he created for the class celebration: a memory book containing 100 family photographs. So when his friends arrive at school with their projects—100 paper clips, 100 marbles, 100 bottle caps, and so forth—Jake is devastated. The principal, Mrs. Wadsworth, comes to the rescue by inviting Jake to assemble 100 picture books from her office, a mere fraction of her collection. The celebration is a success, topped off by a surprise visit from Jake's Aunt Lula, who is 100 years old! Laminack offers a heartfelt story of the power of classroom community—one that is guaranteed to hold your students' attention from start to finish. If you're looking for a straightforward narrative with a strong beginning, middle, and end, look no further than *Jake's 100th Day of School*.

A Color of His Own

Leo Lionni, Author and Illustrator

Pantheon Books, 1975

Lionni has a knack for telling simple stories with rich messages—messages that resonate with children and get them thinking, talking, and, indeed, writing. *A Color of His Own* is no exception. It's the story of a little chameleon that is saddened by the realization that he will never have a color of his own because his color continually changes to match his surroundings. That is, until he meets a wise older friend who agrees to accompany him wherever he goes and change colors along with him. Lionni's vibrant illustrations drive the book's organization; we're right there with the chameleon as he shifts from yellow to purple to polka-dotted. As such, this is the perfect mentor text for children who love to tell stories through drawing. For all children, it sends a message that what's important is not what we are on the outside, but who we are on the inside.

Stand Tall, Molly Lou Melon

Patty Lovell, Author

David Catrow, Illustrator

G. P. Putnam's Sons, 2001

Something as simple as the refrain can work wonderfully as the pivotal organizational device in a story. In this sweet piece, it's "And so she did." Molly Lou gets teased by the other children a lot, but her grandmother reminds her at every turn to walk proudly, stand tall, and smile big. And when Molly Lou moves to a new town and school where she doesn't have her grandmother to fall back on, she realizes that she needs to find the strength within herself to be unique and make her own way in her new life. And so she does.

My Grandmother's Clock

Geraldine McCaughrean, Author

Stephen Lambert, Illustrator

Clarion Books, 2002

How do we measure time? Most of us would answer, "By looking at a clock." But McCaughrean challenges that assumption with this sumptuous story of a little girl who wonders why her grandmother never gets around to fixing the broken grandfather clock in her hallway. Her grandmother responds, "Why…when I have so many other clocks telling me the time?" But these are not clocks she buys in stores. They are the clocks that sustain her and rule her universe: the beating of her heart, the blinking of her eyes, the singing of the birds at dawn, the setting of the sun at dusk, the arrival and departure of seasons. McCaughrean ingeniously organizes the book according to time span, beginning with seconds and moving on to minutes, hours, days, weeks, months, years, and, finally, centuries. This is a book about time for all time.

I Wanna Iguana

Karen Kaufman Orloff, Author

David Catrow, Illustrator

Putnam, 2004

Alex is a typical kid who plays soccer, despises his little brother, and wants a pet more than anything in the world. But it's not a dog, cat, or bird that he wants. He wants an iguana, much to his mother's dismay. So he writes a series of letters to his mother, explaining all the reasons an iguana is the perfect pet for him. And she writes letters back to him, explaining all the reasons one isn't. This is a hilarious and heartwarming story—one that will draw in your students for many reasons: Orloff's authentic voice, Alex's believable quandary, and Catrow's unbelievable illustrations that depict Alex's imagined life with a six-foot iguana! Your students will learn about the power of writing to persuade even the most stubborn mother or father. And they will thank you, for sure. Their parents, however, may not! See focus lesson, pages 35–36.

The Tortilla Factory

Gary Paulsen, Author

Ruth Wright Paulsen, Illustrator

Harcourt Brace & Company, 1995

"The black earth sleeps in winter. But in the spring the black earth is worked by brown hands." And so begins this story of how tortillas, a staple in so many American kitchens, are made. We follow farmers in the field, preparing the soil, planting the seeds, and growing the corn. We follow workers in the factory, using corn flour to create dough, kneading the dough, and baking it into tortillas. Finally, we return to the farmers at home, eating the tortillas, nourishing themselves so that they can continue their work. In other words, the story comes full circle—like life itself. This book works on many levels. It is a wonderful example of narrative nonfiction. It is a wonderful example of poetic language. But mostly it is a testament to the importance of honoring the earth and appreciating what it brings us every day. See focus lesson, pages 37–38.

The Great Gracie Chase: Stop That Dog!

Cynthia Rylant, Author
Mark Teague, Illustrator
Scholastic, 2001

Rylant is a writer of many colors. She is as adept at writing thoughtful young adult novels (e.g., *Missing May*) as she is at delightful chapter books (e.g., the Henry and Mudge series) and whimsical picture books such as this one. Gracie is a little dog who loves her quiet house in a big way. So when the painters arrive to paint the kitchen, rattling ladders, dragging furniture, and shouting to one another, Gracie doesn't like it one bit—and gives the painters a piece of her mind by barking at them incessantly. So one of the painters escorts her outside. Problem solved, right? Wrong. Another one of the painters left the gate open—and Gracie escapes. The chase is on! Neighbors, the paperboy, the garbageman, and others try to stop her, but with no success. It's a modern-day adaptation of *The Gingerbread Man*, but with a much happier ending.

What's Up, What's Down?

Lola M. Schaefer, Author
Barbara Bash, Illustrator
Greenwillow Books, 2002

Divided into two parts, this book asks, "What's up?" from the perspective of a mole under the earth who looks at roots, grass, trees, and, finally, open sky, and "What's down?" from a perspective that starts above the planet and ends on the ocean floor. The organization of this book is simple and logical, making it easy for students to create their own "What's Up, What's Down?" books.

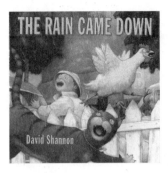

The Rain Came Down

David Shannon, Author and Illustrator

Scholastic, 2000

The author does a nice job of using cause and effect to organize this imaginative story. It is simple, clear, and right to the point. The illustrations are exaggerated, imaginative, and playful—adding greatly to the depth of the piece. Shannon has a style all his own, and his books would be interesting to examine as a group for an author study. If you live in a rainy area, you'll love this book. If you don't, well, you'll see what you are missing!

The Secret Shortcut

Mark Teague, Author and Illustrator

Scholastic, 1996

It's hard not to love this book. It's filled with energy and invites the reader to experience the adventures of the characters right along with them, from beginning to end. Nicely organized, this book shows how to use sequence words to move the reader through the story with ease. After students have enjoyed the story and are ready to flex their organizational writing muscles, ask them to write their own stories.

The Z Was Zapped: A Play in Twenty-Six Acts

Chris Van Allsburg, Author and Illustrator

Houghton Mifflin Company, 1987

Using the alphabet as the organizer, Van Allsburg presents action sentences for each letter to create a story in 26 acts. This clever organizational structure may inspire students to write their own stories in multiple acts using the letters of their names. The excellent use of active verbs is worth noticing and discussing as well.

Scaredy Squirrel

Mélanie Watt, Author and Illustrator

Kids Can Press, 2006

Franklin D. Roosevelt's statement "The only thing we have to fear is fear itself" may have soothed a nation, but it didn't do a thing for Scaredy Squirrel because he is afraid of everything—particularly germs, sharks, tarantulas, poison ivy, killer bees, and green Martians.

So he never strays from his nut tree and always follows the same safe routines. That is, until the day he is visited by an unwelcome guest and, while diving for his emergency kit, makes a surprising discovery about himself. Watt's interplay of text and visuals is fascinating. She combines elements of fiction (plot, characters, etc.) with elements of nonfiction (charts, diagrams, etc.), proving that good organization is not only achieved through words, sentences, and paragraphs. Writing can be organized in all kinds of ways—and thoroughly entertain readers. Check out her equally entertaining follow-up, *Scaredy Squirrel Makes a Friend*, too. See focus lesson, pages 39–40.

Courage

Bernard Waber, Author and Illustrator

Houghton Mifflin Company, 2002

Courage is something we can all use these days—courage to deal with little things like jumping off the high dive, and courage to deal with big things like learning how to say good-bye. Organized around that one simple yet profound word, this book moves from example to example of courage in action. "Courage is riding your bike the first time without training wheels." "Courage is a blade of grass breaking through the icy snow." Wonderful. And it all comes together in the end with a universal message—"Courage is what we give to each other." We take this book with us as we travel around the country and meet teachers, because teachers are courageous people. We hope this book reminds you of that!

Bear Snores On

Karma Wilson, Author

Jane Chapman, Illustrator

Margaret K. McElderry Books, 2002

Deep in the woods on a cold, snowy night, a great brown bear sleeps soundly in his cave—so soundly, in fact, even seven shelter-seeking outsiders don't rouse him. First a mouse arrives and builds a fire, but the bear snores on. Then a hare arrives and pops some corn, but the bear snores on. Then a badger, gopher, mole, raven, and wren join them. The party has begun. But the bear snores on. That is, until a rogue pepper flake finds its way into the bear's nose, and—"RAAAAA-CHOOOOOO!"—he wakes up. He's angry not because he has been inundated by squatters, but because he has slept through all the fun. That is until the mouse assures him that there's still plenty of time for that. This is a top-notch book largely because of its organization. Wilson keeps the momentum going by introducing a quirky critter on each page spread and ends on a deeply satisfying note.

THREE FOCUS LESSONS ON ORGANIZATION

LESSON 1

I Wanna Iguana

Karen Kaufman Orloff, Author

David Catrow, Illustrator

Putnam, 2004

TARGET TRAIT: ORGANIZATION

There's no end to the reasons young Alex gives his mother for why he should have an iguana as a pet. But Mom has her own reasons why she's not too keen on that idea. This book shows students how to organize ideas for a personal letter or series of notes—and makes them laugh out loud in the process. Students learn to include a greeting, body, and a closing as part of the letter-writing format and, as an added bonus, they get to try their hand at writing in the persuasive mode.

MATERIALS:

❈ a copy of *I Wanna Iguana*

❈ chart paper

❈ paper

❈ pencils, pens

❈ a willing principal

WHAT TO DO:

1. Read the book, showing the pictures and letters as you go.

2. Ask students to tell you what they enjoyed most about the book. Reread individual pages so they can hear them again and get a clear sense of Orloff's style.

3. Tell students they will be learning how to write letters like those in Orloff's book.

4. On chart paper, write out one of the letters from the text, showing the greeting, body, closing, and P.S. Label each part clearly.

5. Ask students to think of what the opposite of a snow day would be—how about a "sun day"? Make a list of all the things they could do to celebrate a day of sunshine and fun: running field activities, making ice cream, sharing books and magazines at story hour, having water balloon races, eating grilled hot dogs and hamburgers, and so on.

6. If students like the idea, ask them to help you write a letter to the principal proposing an all-school "sun day" for a date in the spring. Start by brainstorming ideas for the letter on chart paper. Point out where the greeting, body, closing, and P.S. go as you help them organize their letter.

7. Ask a student to fold the letter, address it to the principal, and take it to him or her.

8. Behind the scenes, discuss with your principal the idea you have for creating an all-school "sun day." If planning a schoolwide activity is more than the principal wishes to commit to, you can modify this activity to be only a classroom-based "sun day." Give the principal a copy of *I Wanna Iguana* to use for ideas in his or her responses to the class's letter. Ask the principal to participate by writing back to the students several times as they negotiate the details of "sun day."

9. Ask for a response to the class letter within three days. If possible, have the principal write his or her letter on chart paper, too, so it is big enough for all the children to see.

10. Write letters back and forth at least five times, coming up with new ideas for why the principal should honor the request for a "sun day" each time. Post all the letters around the room. If students are able, they can begin writing personal letters to the principal.

11. Once the principal agrees to a "sun day" for the school, have the students write individual thank-you notes to him or her, assuring the principal that they will be responsible and help with the setup and cleanup.

12. Schedule the event for spring. Plan with the class and the rest of the school how to organize the day so it is fun, interesting, and instructional.

FOLLOW-UP ACTIVITIES:

❋ Take photos on "sun day" and share them with parents in a newsletter.

❋ Read and enjoy another book organized around a series of letters from a child to an adult, *Dear Mr. Blueberry* by Simon James. Show how this book also contains the key elements of a letter.

The Tortilla Factory

Gary Paulsen, Author
Ruth Wright Paulsen, Illustrator
Harcourt Brace & Company, 1995

TARGET TRAIT:
ORGANIZATION

You can pick out the organization of this elegant text quite easily: it's a cycle—the cycle of planting, harvesting, and processing grain to make tortillas. Primary students will appreciate how carefully Paulsen writes about this cycle since the entire text is one sentence that clearly illustrates the tortilla-making process, beginning to end. In this lesson, students examine the organizational structure of the text and make connections to other cyclical processes in the world.

MATERIALS:

❉ a copy of *The Tortilla Factory*

❉ an overhead of the book's beginning and ending text:

Beginning: . . . in the spring the black earth is worked by brown hands that plant yellow seeds, which become green plants rustling in soft wind and make golden corn to dry in hot sun and be ground into flour for the tortilla factory. . .

Ending: . . . and give strength to the brown hands that work the black earth to plant yellow seeds, which make golden corn to be dried in hot sun and be ground into flour. . . .

❉ chart paper or posterboard

❉ 3″ x 3″ squares of drawing paper

❉ pens, markers, crayons

❉ glue

WHAT TO DO:

1. Read the book aloud to students and let them enjoy Paulsen's fine language and vivid imagery.

2. Ask if anyone noticed anything interesting or unusual in the way the book was organized. Remind them that organization is how the ideas are laid out by the author, what comes first, second, third, and so on.

3. Show the beginning and ending of the book on the overhead so students can see the pattern used by the author.

4. When the organization of this book is fully discussed, ask students to give it a name: a cycle, a full circle, or other synonym.

5. Ask students to help you make a list of other things in the world that happen in cycles. Write these on the chart paper or poster board so all can see:

    *   water cycle
    *   seasons
    *   life
    *   school
    *   summer vacation
    *   the days and nights
    *   plants and trees

6. Give each student a small piece of paper and crayons, markers, or colored pencils and ask them to draw a picture of one of the cycles that you just talked about.

7. Lay out all the pictures, group similar ones together, and paste them onto posterboard or chart paper.

8. Ask students to label each cluster, such as "The Seasons" or "The School Year."

9. Write "Cycles" at the top and hang your organization poster for all to see.

FOLLOW-UP ACTIVITIES:

*   Ask students to discuss other instances in which writers might use cyclical organization. Invite them to consider TV shows and movies that begin the story in one place, then feature flashbacks to tell the whole story from beginning to end.

*   Share other favorite books that are organized cyclically, such as *If You Give a Pig a Pancake* by Laura Numeroff.

LESSON 3

Scaredy Squirrel
Mélanie Watt, Author and Illustrator
Kids Can Press, 2006

TARGET TRAIT: ORGANIZATION

Scaredy Squirrel goes to great lengths to keep his life in order, documenting his fears about change, things that terrify him, his daily schedule, and the advantages and disadvantages of leaving his nut tree. Scaredy even explains what he keeps in an emergency kit and steps to take in case the worst should happen—such as leaving the nut tree! In this lesson, students create their own lists, schedules, plans, and charts as they zero in on the organization of nonfiction writing using this sweet and lively book as a model.

MATERIALS:

✳ a copy of *Scaredy Squirrel*

✳ slips of paper

✳ a box or hat

✳ chart paper, pens, and markers

WHAT TO DO:

1. Read *Scaredy Squirrel* to the class.

2. Brainstorm with the class a list of things Scaredy Squirrel writes about that show his personality: a) his greatest fears, b) advantages and disadvantages of change (leaving the nut tree), c) his daily routine, d) contents of an emergency kit, and e) an exit plan for an emergency.

3. Discuss the ways each type of writing in the book is organized:

   ✳ a list of items on a common topic

   ✳ a chart comparing two items to show differences or similarities

   ✳ a schedule or timeline

   ✳ a step-by-step plan to solve a problem

4. Write each type of organization on a slip of paper and put into a box or hat.

5. Put the students into small groups and have one person from each group draw a slip and read it to the group. This will be the organization for their group writing to come next. Put the slips of paper back in the box before the next group draws so all groups have the same options.

6. Ask each group to come up with a new list, chart, schedule, or plan, depending on what their slip says: a) things they do well in school, b) things they like and don't like about going to school, c) a schedule of their school day, or d) a step-by-step plan to get out of the classroom in case of an emergency. Give students time to record their writing on chart paper and ask them to draw pictures to illustrate their ideas.

7. Share what each group wrote and how members organized their ideas. Compare the differences and similarities of how each piece is organized.

FOLLOW-UP ACTIVITIES:

❖ Discuss with students what makes the organization of writing such as that found in *Scaredy Squirrel* different from a story or good information book. Emphasize the different ways to organize for different purposes to make the ideas stand out.

❖ Share the sequel to *Scaredy Squirrel*, *Scaredy Squirrel Makes a Friend* by Mélanie Watt, and discuss how it is organized.

CHAPTER 3

Sparking Voice

Voice is the energy of the writing that creates a strong reader-writer interaction. It's how we know the author feels strongly about the subject. It's the writer's distinctive fingerprint that makes the writing his or her own. In the work of the youngest writers, the voice may show up in the detail in pictures, the use of punctuation (many exclamation points, for instance), and the size of the letters to show emphasis. To be successful with the voice trait, primary students need practice with the following:

* finding voice

* matching voice to purpose

* discovering new voices

As you read and discuss the books in this section, talk with students about the reactions they have to the texts. Ask them to name the emotions or feelings that each of these pieces make them feel. And most importantly, make sure your students understand that their writing needs to connect with the reader, too.

VOICE: A DEFINITION FOR PRIMARY STUDENTS

Sparkling, confident, unquestionably individual. These are words that describe a piece of writing with voice. Voice is the writer's passion for the topic coming through loud and clear. It's what keeps us turning the pages of a story long after bedtime. It's what makes an essay about camels fascinating, even though we didn't think we cared all that much about camels. Voice is what primary writers use to assert their own way of looking at an idea. You'll find it in scribbles, in their letter strings, in their sentences, and in their continuous text. Voice can permeate writing, regardless of where the writer falls on the developmental continuum. Primary writers are well on their way to applying voice when they exhibit the following:

* have something important to say

* create drawings that are expressive

* find new ways of expressing familiar ideas

* capture a range of emotions, from gleeful to poignant to afraid

* offer sincere thoughts

* are confident that what they say matters

* demonstrate awareness of an audience

* are willing to take a risk and try something that no classmate has tried before

* apply original thinking

PICTURE BOOKS FOR SPARKING VOICE

Train to Somewhere

Eve Bunting, Author

Ronald Himler, Illustrator

Clarion Books, 1996

Too frequently, teachers don't begin introducing historical fiction until the upper elementary grades. We believe that's a mistake. Children in the primary grades want, need, and deserve to learn about people and events of the past—and there are some wonderful picture books available to teach them, including *Train to Somewhere*. From the mid-1850s to the late 1920s, thousands of orphaned children from New York City were escorted west by train, seeking permanent, loving homes. Some were successful, others were not. *Train to Somewhere* is the fictionalized account of one of those journeys, told by Marianne, an older child whose chances of finding a home are marginal at best. Bunting's interpretation of Marianne's voice is pitch perfect, capturing all the fear, grief, and hope that these children most certainly felt.

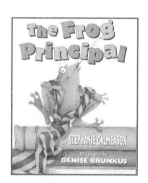

The Frog Principal

Stephanie Calmenson, Author

Denise Brunkus, Illustrator

Scholastic, 2001

Remember the story of the Frog Prince told by the Brothers Grimm? This time it's the assistant principal who is the frog, and, oh, what a hard time the children have with him. Their principal "goes away" and in his place comes a slimy, green frog. What happens next is funny and original, and the voice is delightful. It's a nice example of how an author can write a funny piece without overwriting it. This twist on a familiar story should inspire young writers to come up with their own versions.

Little Yau: A Fuzzhead Tale

Janell Cannon, Author and Illustrator

Harcourt, Inc., 2002

Heartfelt, sweet, compassionate. With this book, Cannon scores big in voice. How can a reader resist Little Yau and the other Fuzzheads when most of the book is the search for an herb to cure one of their own who lies dying? And, when the search takes them into the land of people, you have to hold your breath and hope that it will all turn out well. Several intermingled themes work well here—friendship, growing up, and child-adult relationships.

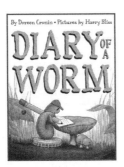

Diary of a Worm

Doreen Cronin, Author

Harry Bliss, Illustrator

Joanna Cotler Books, 2003

The insights about life told through this little earthworm's writing is guaranteed to tickle you and your students. In one of our favorite passages, the worm tells his vain older sister that she's wasting her time gazing at herself in the mirror because her face looks just like her rear end. In another, when he decides to use good manners, he winds up saying "good morning" to six hundred ants. Whew! That's a lot. From the first page to the last, Cronin captures this charming little earthworm's voice as she parallels the everyday lives of humans and insects.

Ice Bear: In the Steps of the Polar Bear

Nicola Davies, Author

Gary Blythe, Illustrator

Candlewick Press, 2005

Ice Bear is a fine example of just how far informational text for children has come. The narrator, an Inuit person, explains the characteristics and habits of the polar bear—or "nanuk," as her people call it—in the most respectful, reverent terms. Take, for instance, how she describes the play of two male bears: "They'll wave their heads in greeting, clasp jaws so tenderly, they wouldn't break an egg. Cautiously, they'll try each other's strength. Then? Play! Giants flowing in the whiteness, tumbling, beautiful as snowflakes...." We learn so much about these majestic animals because Davies has done her homework and writes from her head and heart. And Blythe's oil-and-pencil illustrations capture the polar bear's daily life brilliantly, whether she's hunting alone in the frozen Arctic landscape or nursing a cub in her safe, warm den.

Surprising Sharks

Nicola Davies, Author

James Croft, Illustrator

Candlewick Press, 2003

Some informational texts enlighten, some engage, and some entertain. Surprising Sharks hits a bull's eye by doing all three. Davies serves up a banquet of fun, fascinating facts about sharks, addressing their physical characteristics (Did you know that full-grown sharks can be as small as 6 inches and as large as 39 feet?) and habits (Did you know that sharks kill only about six people a year? You're more likely to be done in by a dog!). What makes the book so strong, though, is Davies's voice. Her fascination and enthusiasm for sharks lift off every page, and Croft's crazy, colorful illustrations compliment her witty observations perfectly. The book also contains a ton of useful, well-researched information that can be used in reports, projects, and playground conversation. Your students will love sinking their teeth into this book!

Always and Forever

Alan Durant, Author
Debi Gliori, Illustrator
Harcourt, Inc., 2003

Few topics are more difficult to talk about with a child than death. But it's an important topic, certainly worth addressing, especially if that child has lost someone special. Picture books can get the conversation going. It's almost impossible for a writer to address the topic without voice—without some level of sadness, terror, anger, relief, or any other emotion that death typically conjures. Alan Durant proves this with *Always and Forever*, the story of a woodland animal family that loses a beloved member, Fox. Despair rules the household until Squirrel visits and reminds everyone of the healing power of good memories. If you're considering sharing this book with your students, expect some tough questions and responses. But don't let that stop you because, as teachers, we all know this is a fertile starting point for great writing.

Yesterday I Had the Blues

Jeron Ashford Frame, Author
R. Gregory Christie, Illustrator
Tricycle Press, 2003

To a large extent, writing with voice means writing with emotion. A young mother's memoir about having a baby may be joyful. A commuter's editorial about rising gasoline prices may be angry. A soldier's letter from the front lines may be cheerful, but tinged with sadness and even fear. *Yesterday I Had the Blues* is full of emotion, as described by a young boy who starts out with the blues, but winds up with the "greens" (hopeful). But his daddy has the "grays" (tense), his mama has the "reds" (annoyed), his sister has the "pinks" (cheerful), and so forth. By the end, we realize what the boy truly has is a real family with real feelings. Read this book to your students. Talk to them about times they've had the blues, as well as the greens, grays, reds, pinks, and so forth. Then ask them to put their ideas on paper. You'll be amazed at how colorful their voices can be. See focus lesson, pages 52–53.

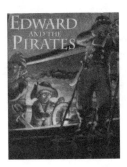

Edward and the Pirates

David McPhail, Author and Illustrator

Little, Brown, 1997

Never forget the power of books to let our imaginations soar. That is the message of *Edward and the Pirates*. Edward discovers that reading can take him anywhere—from racing dog sleds with Admiral Peary to running from the Sheriff of Nottingham in Sherwood Forest. One night in Edward's dreams, pirates come to life and tell him to hand over the book he is reading; they think it will tell them where their buried treasure lies. But, sadly, because the pirates don't know how to read, the book won't do them much good. As Edward helps them, they discover together that the real treasure is knowing how to read.

Steal Back the Mona Lisa!

Meghan McCarthy, Author and Illustrator

Harcourt, Inc., 2006

For most children, "capturing bad guys" is a favorite make-believe activity. Since the birth of Superman himself, little crime fighters have been nabbing kidnappers, muggers, and bank robbers blissfully, without ever leaving their bedrooms. That's why we're confident that children will love this book about the theft of the Mona Lisa, and one boy's mission to retrieve it. McCarthy's illustrations are wildly witty, taking us from the United States to Russia and finally to France. We follow the boy as he travels by car, plane, and boat, using a whole range of crime-stopping gadgets inspired by classic James Bond movies. But what will really grab and hold students' attention is McCarthy's writing. She uses a question-and-answer format, laced with unexpected twists and turns, that will get kids wondering, laughing, and wanting more.

Straight to the Pole

Kevin O'Malley, Author and Illustrator

Walker Publishing Company, Inc., 2003

Straight to the Pole—the first-person account of a young child trudging through a snowstorm to some undisclosed place—proves that a writer doesn't need to use a lot of words to achieve a lot of voice. For the most part, O'Malley uses short, clipped phrases, and not full sentences, to capture what the child is saying: "Pushing through wind. Over hills and mountains. Slipping. Sliding. Bone chilling wind biting my cheeks. I can't go on." By doing so, he achieves a level of authenticity to which most students will undoubtedly relate. As the child plugs on, we can't help but plug on right alongside him. By the end, we realize that he is on his way to one of the most mundane places in the world: the school-bus stop. This is an excellent example of how using one's senses— describing not only how a situation looks, but also how it *feels*—can bring writing to life. See focus lesson, pages 53–54.

Earthquack!
Margie Palatini, Author

Barry Moser, Illustrator

Simon & Schuster Books for Young Readers, 2002

Little Chucky Ducky has just finished his laps around the pond, dried off his bill, and let the water roll off his back. It's a typical morning, in other words. That is, until the earth starts wobbling beneath his webbed feet and he sets off on a mad dash to warn his barnyard friends, one by one, that they are in grave danger. "The earth is crumbling! The earth is crumbling! Why, it's a quake," he quacks. But are they really in danger? Or is something far more harmless happening? Palatini has created a masterful modern-day *Henny Penny*, using wonderful wordplay reminiscent of Arnold Adoff and John Ciardi. Moser's watercolors capture the chaos magnificently. As such, *Earthquack!* is one of those picture books that was born to be read aloud to—and thoroughly enjoyed by—children everywhere.

The Mighty Asparagus
V. Radunsky, Author and Illustrator

Harcourt, Inc., 2004

Something quite amazing has happened in the kingdom: A gigantic asparagus has sprung up out of nowhere smack dab in the middle of the courtyard—and the king is not happy. He finds the asparagus "ugly," "smelly," and completely unacceptable. So he recruits his wife, daughter, bravest knight, and beloved rhinoceros to drop the dreaded stock and drag it away. Bad idea. The asparagus is, indeed, much too mighty for them all. But it isn't too mighty for a tiny bird that topples it with a flutter of its wings. This book's design is as amazing as the story itself—a mad montage of Italian Renaissance paintings and Redunsky's own renditions of the royals and their loyal subjects. And his voice comes through loud and clear, dripping with riotous reflections, insights, and opinions, as he reports on the extraordinary event.

Red Rubber Boot Day

Mary Lyn Ray, Author

Lauren Stringer, Illustrator

Harcourt, Inc., 2000

While rainy days can be just plain miserable to us adults, they can be magical to children, as *Red Rubber Boot Day* demonstrates. In it, we shadow a young boy as he considers a whole host of indoor activities: "I may read. I like to read when it rains. I may play cars. Or cave. My best cave is my closet." But in time, he dashes out the door, in his favorite red rubber boots, to splash in puddles. Glorious puddles! "I like slapping, stirring puddles. I like a day for boots." Your students will relate to this book not only because the boy is engaging in activities they typically do, but also because he speaks in language they typically use. The narrative is so natural. It actually sounds like a young child talking—and, as you know as a primary teacher, young children speak with tremendous voice.

Ish

Peter H. Reynolds, Author and Illustrator

Candlewick Press, 2004

Ramon loves to draw. That is, until his older brother ridicules one of his creations, a picture of flowers in a vase, and destroys Ramon's confidence. Fortunately, his younger sister has a better eye. While she admits his drawing isn't perfect, she feels it's "vase-ish." In fact, she sees "ish" in all of Ramon's work, which covers her bedroom walls. In time, Ramon himself sees "ish" in his work, and finds it liberating because "thinking ishly" allows his ideas to flow freely. Reynolds's voice is encouraging and energizing. In essence, he's telling his readers that being creative requires taking risks. Whether we're writing a poem, composing a song, or, like Ramon, drawing a picture, we must move beyond our safety zone to create something deeply satisfying to our audience and ourselves. We ask, is there a more important message to send to students? See focus lesson, pages 55–56.

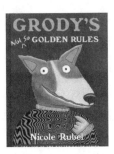

Grody's Not So Golden Rules

Nicole Rubel, Author and Illustrator

Harcourt, Inc., 2003

Tongue in cheek from beginning to end, this book is a delightful twist on the rules that many children live by every day. Little Grody turns motherly "suggestions," such as "You'd better straighten up your room," into more acceptable ones: "Don't bother putting your clothes away. They will be easier to find if you leave them out!" All children will enjoy Grody's version of the rules, and will want to add a few of their own!

In November

Cynthia Rylant, Author

Jill Kastner, Illustrator

Harcourt Brace, 2000

"In November, the earth is growing quiet. It is making its bed, a winter bed…." Thus begins Cynthia Rylant's forceful book about the forces of nature. The chill arrives. Snow covers the earth. And all living things band together for comfort and protection.

Rylant opens by addressing animals—how bees burrow in the earth, cats huddle in the barn, some birds fly south (while others remain behind despite the approaching freeze). From there, she addresses humans—how we, too, band together, warm and safe inside our homes, nourishing one another, nurturing one another. Rylant's voice is sensitive and, at the same time, authoritative; the reader learns a thing or two about wildlife and how it prepares for winter. But what we like most about this book is what Rylant doesn't state—that life is dynamic, fleeting, and sacred. We must cherish every moment.

The Relatives Came

Cynthia Rylant, Author

Stephen Gammell, Illustrator

Aladdin Paperbacks, 1985

Summer vacation carries with it a feel and texture all its own. This book captures that mood, tone, and voice of these carefree days. When relatives come to visit, we experience the joy of family vacations, somehow forgetting things like age-old squabbles, the insufferable cousin, and the smelly dog. We appreciate what's really important about families as the author relates this story about a time when relatives, young and old, unite in hugs and laughter.

Beverly Billingsly Takes a Bow

Alexander Stadler, Author and Illustrator

Harcourt, Inc., 2003

Imagine the horror that Beverly feels when, while trying out for the school play, she opens her mouth and nothing comes out. Given a smaller part with only one line, Beverly is more than ready to give it her best on opening night. However, her most shining moment comes when she bravely steps in for a classmate who comes down with a bad case of stage fright. Her empathy for her friend and a thoughtful gift just when it is needed make Beverly Billingsly a very lovable character. In this simple story, Stadler uses a sweet and compassionate voice to show us the meaning of true friendship.

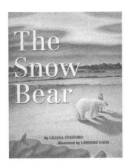

The Snow Bear

Liliana Stafford, Author

Lambert Davis, Illustrator

Scholastic, 2000

This story of a boy and a polar bear is simply told. The reality of their life in the Inuit village—how villagers must hunt bears to survive—is not sugar-coated. The voice is authentic because the author truly knows the ways of the Inuit natives. We were struck by how beautiful a person this protagonist is—real and kind. Brunn befriends a starving bear, and they learn to live together in the wild. Years later, Brunn runs into the bear again. Starving and old, Brunn is faced with the choice of killing the bear or helping him survive one last winter. When we turned the final page, we took a deep breath.

My Big Dog

Janet Stevens and Susan Stevens Crummel, Authors

Janet Stevens, Illustrator

Golden Books, 1999

Point of view is a key consideration in voice. And from the title, you probably assume that this story is told from the point of view of the owner of a big dog. But in reality, it's told from a cat's point of view—a cat named Meryl whose perfect life is disrupted by a wiggly, noisy, slurpy, and clumsy puppy. Imagine the disdain of the cat who had everything—dish, sofa, chair, toy mouse, and bed—adjusting to this unwelcome addition to the family. After trying everything to get rid of the dog, Meryl has no choice but to leave. What follows is a series of events that eventually brings the cat back asking the question, "Could we be friends?"

The Little Red Hen (Makes a Pizza)

Philemon Sturges, Author

Amy Walrod, Illustrator

Dutton Children's Books, 1999

Lively, funny, and clever, this little red hen makes a pizza with about as much help as the original little red hen who made the bread. Contemporary but true to the classic story, this book will delight students and adults with the timeless message of working in cooperation to meet shared goals. The ending brings a charming surprise. You might want to compare and contrast voice in the two versions of the story.

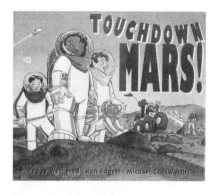

Touchdown Mars!

Peggy Wethered and Ken Edgett, Authors

Michael Chesworth, Illustrator

G. P. Putnam's Sons, 2000

Written in two voices, one expressive and one more academic, this book is good for helping students see how important it is to have a clear sense of purpose and audience when they write. Each page has two effective styles blending narrative and expository texts to create a voice that is both factually credible and fascinating to read. This would be an interesting format for students to try in their own writing.

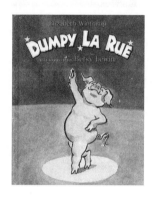

Dumpy La Rue

Elizabeth Winthrop, Author

Betsy Lewin, Illustrator

Henry Holt and Company, 2001

What do you do with a pig that wants to dance? You let him, of course! That's the happy ending for Dumpy La Rue. But he doesn't get to dance until he convinces his parents and all the other barnyard animals that wanting to dance isn't strange. It is fun. A pig ought to be able to do what he wants and what he's good at, right? This darling story is affirming for children. It helps them to realize that if they take a risk and try something different, it's more than okay. This is the same understanding that writers need to embrace to have voice in their writing. It's the only way to go for them and for Dumpy La Rue, the pig who knew what he wanted to do.

THREE FOCUS LESSONS ON VOICE

LESSON 1

Yesterday I Had the Blues

Jeron Ashford Frame, Author
R. Gregory Christie, Illustrator
Tricycle Press, 2003

TARGET TRAIT: VOICE

This lively book is about a boy and his family. Each page introduces a new character by pairing color with mood: red for annoyed; pink for spunky; blue for depressed; and so forth. As you read, it's easy to hear the author's voice as he shares insider information on each family member. Students will enjoy thinking about how color is associated with their own personality characteristics and moods. For this lesson, they will pick colors and explain, using fun and interesting details as modeled in the book, why the color fits them perfectly.

MATERIALS:

❊ a copy of *Yesterday I Had the Blues*

❊ paper

❊ pencils, crayons, markers

❊ optional: magazines as a source of pictures

WHAT TO DO:

1. Ask students to think about their mood when they woke up. Were they in a good mood, looking forward to going to school? Or were they in a bad mood, wishing they could roll over and go back to sleep? Perhaps they were feeling yet another way?

2. Tell them to talk to a partner about their mood and select a color that matches it. If they were happy, for instance, they might pick bright green or yellow. If they were sad, they might choose gray, brown, or black. Encourage them to match their mood to a color as closely as they can.

3. Read *Yesterday I Had the Blues* to the class, showing the pictures as you go.

4. Ask students to name the mood of each character and how they identified it. Their answers should include the color the author used as well as his description of the character.

5. Ask students to talk to their partner again about the mood they were in when they got ready for school and to refine their thoughts based on *Yesterday I Had the Blues*.

6. Ask students to write about and illustrate on paper their mood, explaining the color they think best reflects that mood and why they chose it.

7. Share the mood pieces with the class and discuss them. Explain to students that writing should capture mood, or voice, to help the reader feel what the writer is feeling.

FOLLOW-UP ACTIVITIES:

❈ Help students create a book of colors and moods. Print lists of colors from the Internet and ask students to attach a mood to each one. Then bind the lists as a book for students to consult when they write.

❈ Share *The Sound of Colors: A Journey of the Imagination* by Jimmy Liao and discuss how the author describes colors. Ask students to discuss the book's voice and how color helped them to identify that voice.

LESSON 2

Straight to the Pole
Kevin O'Malley, Author and Illustrator
Walker Publishing Company, Inc., 2003

TARGET TRAIT: VOICE

This account of a young boy's struggle to make it to the school-bus stop during a blizzard is bound to make students howl with laughter. Featuring short, emphatic phrases such as "I'm doomed" and "Must . . . go . . . on," to exaggerate the seriousness of the situation, the book is a delight from the first to the last page. Students will enjoy reading it over and over, adding a dramatic flair to capture the character of the protagonist. In this lesson, students work together to create a poster of how O'Malley creates strong voice, which can be expanded over time as students examine how other authors also use voice.

MATERIALS:

❈ a copy of *Straight to the Pole*

❈ posterboard

❈ paper

❈ pens, markers

❈ scissors

WHAT TO DO:

1. Discuss with students that writers use a quality called voice to give their writing character and make it memorable to the reader.

2. Ask students to recall favorite books and see if they can identify the voice in a single word. For example, if they choose books by Dr. Seuss, they might identify the voice as "silly." If they choose books by Eve Bunting, they might say "serious."

3. Tell students they are going to hear a book that has very strong voice. Ask them to think about words they could use to describe the voice as you read *Straight to the Pole.*

4. Read the book, stopping to share the pictures as you go.

5. When you have finished, ask students if they enjoyed the book. The answer will most likely be "Yes!" Most students think this is a very funny book and aren't hesitant to talk about why. See how many words they can come up with to describe O'Malley's voice: hilarious, silly, outrageous, funny, ridiculous, and so on.

6. Go back through the book with your students, looking for examples of how the author was so successful expressing his idea with so much voice. See how many of the following elements and techniques that students notice:

   ❋ dialogue

   ❋ exaggeration

   ❋ punctuation to show emphasis

   ❋ surprise ending

   ❋ large and smaller print to get the reader's attention

   ❋ short, clipped phrasing

   ❋ other

7. Ask students to pick passages in which O'Malley created voice and write or draw them on paper, cut them out, and post them on a class posterboard entitled: "How to Add Voice to My Writing." Match the passages in the text to the list they created above.

8. Hang the poster up for everyone to see. Revisit the importance of voice and encourage students to refer to the poster any time for ideas of how to add voice to their own pieces.

FOLLOW-UP ACTIVITIES:

❋ As students hear and read other books containing strong voice, have them add new examples to the poster.

❋ Ask the librarian to collect other O'Malley books, including *Bruno, You're Late for School*; *Once Upon a Cool Motorcycle Dude*; *Herbert Fieldmouse, Secret Agent*; *Velcome*; and *Humpty Dumpty Egg-Splodes* and give them to a small group to read. Ask students to determine if all of O'Malley's books are written in a funny voice or if some are written in other kinds of voices.

Ish

Peter H. Reynolds, Author and Illustrator
Candlewick Press, 2004

TARGET TRAIT: VOICE

It's easy to get discouraged when you're trying to learn something difficult. Ramon finds this out firsthand when he tries to draw a vase but his pictures don't turn out the way he wants. After many tries, he gives up, crumpling his paper and throwing it across the room. His sister, Marisol, retrieves the drawing and hangs it in her room, along with others by Ramon she has collected. Marisol tells him that she likes the drawing even though it's imperfect—or in her words, "vase-ish." Ramon finds his artistic voice as he begins to draw again, and that voice begins to show up in his writing, too. Being "ish" frees him to be himself. In this lesson, students try their hand at writing "ish" poems, describing how it feels to be new at something such as reading, writing, or any topic of their choice.

MATERIALS:

❊ a copy of *Ish*

❊ overhead and pens

❊ paper

❊ pencils

WHAT TO DO:

1. Read the book to students and discuss how it feels to be a learner. Ask them if they have ever felt frustrated like Ramon, and what they did to overcome that feeling.

2. Explain to students that they will be writing "ish" poems about something they have found challenging to learn. Brainstorm with students possible topics:

   ❊ a subject in school

   ❊ a sport

   ❊ a chore at home

   ❊ a musical instrument

   ❊ personal challenges such as whistling, snapping fingers, tying shoes

3. Choose a skill you found hard to learn, and compose a poem about it on the overhead. Here's an example:

> "Whistle-ish"
> When I was six I blew and blew
> But no cool sound would my lips make
> I tried to whistle, again and again…
> But the noise that came out
> Sounded more like a tornado
> Than the whistle of a train
> I guess you could say I was "whistle-ish"

4. Ask students to choose a partner and write a poem together about something they found hard to learn. Encourage them to express their feelings as best they can.

5. Have students share poems in small groups and with the class.

FOLLOW-UP ACTIVITIES:

✻   Encourage students to draw, just like Ramon. Hang the pictures around the room and ask other students to label what they think the picture is about, reminding them that the pictures will be "ish," and that's not a bad thing.

✻   Read and enjoy *The Dot,* another book by Reynolds that emphasizes the value of individual expression over perfection.

CHAPTER 4

Expanding
Word Choice

The use of just the right word in just the right place is an important goal for writers. It doesn't happen right off the bat, however. When students write their first drafts, their attention should be on capturing the idea, not selecting the exact word or phrase. It's in a second or third pass at the writing that precision with words takes place. To support primary students, we need to help them do the following:

* fall in love with words

* choose precise words

* select words with color, variety, and sparkle

Each of the books in this word choice section was chosen because it has something special to offer. It might be the use of unusual words, striking words, or memorable words and phrases. Or, the author may have done an extraordinary job using everyday words well. Regardless, as you and your students read and enjoy these books, stop to discuss the words and encourage students to try using some of their favorites as they look at their writing and revise the words so they dance and sparkle throughout.

WORD CHOICE: A DEFINITION FOR PRIMARY STUDENTS

When we explore word choice in the classroom, we focus on the parts of speech that writers use to convey meaning—the nouns, verbs, adjectives, adverbs, pronouns, contractions, gerunds, and so on. These terms may conjure up chilling moments from high school English class, but word choice is not about grammar. It's about selecting words carefully to craft fluent sentences and create a lasting image in the reader's mind. We know that primary students are well on their way to making wise word choices when they do the following:

* play with letters to make words

* attempt to write words they have heard

* try new ways of saying things

* express an interest in the role of different parts of speech—nouns, verbs, adjectives, and so forth

* develop a curiosity about language

* use the perfect word in the perfect place

* try sensory words

* use language with precision

PICTURE BOOKS FOR EXPANDING WORD CHOICE

Max's Words
Kate Banks, Author
Boris Kulikov, Illustrator
Farrar, Straus and Giroux, 2006

Max's brother Benjamin collects stamps, and his brother Karl collects coins. But when Max tries to come up with something for himself to collect, he comes up empty. Then he has a brainstorm: words. Max will collect words cut from magazines and newspapers. He begins with small words and moves to bigger ones. Then he categorizes his words: words that make him feel good, things he likes to eat, favorite colors, and so forth. Soon his collection becomes so enormous, he moves it from the desk to the floor—a blank palette for attaching his words to create stories that are so compelling even Benjamin and Karl can't resist helping to draft them. You can build a whole literacy block around this book. Read it aloud and have students find their own favorite words, assemble their words into stories, share their stories, and watch their love for words grow. See focus lesson, pages 68–69.

Things That Are Most in the World
Judi Barrett, Author
John Nickle, Illustrator
Atheneum Books for Young Readers, 1998

What is the smelliest thing in the world? A skunk convention, of course. What is the tiniest thing? A newborn flea, naturally. The jumpiest thing? What else? 2,222 toads on a trampoline! If you want to teach your students about extreme adjectives, or superlatives as they're better known, get a copy of *Things That Are Most in the World*. Barrett organizes the book around a predictable pattern, with her words on the left—"The _____est thing in the world is _____."—and Nickle's colorful, fantastical illustrations on the right, creating the perfect read-aloud book. Your students will not only learn about superlatives, they'll be inspired to apply superlatives to their writing. In fact, to get them started, Barrett includes a handy reproducible page at the back of the book for kids to write about and illustrate their own things that are most in the world. See focus lesson, pages 70–71.

My Teacher Likes to Say

Denise Brennan-Nelson, Author
Jane Monroe Donovan, Illustrator
Sleeping Bear Press, 2004

When teaching about word choice, don't limit yourself to individual words. Teach clichés, idioms, and proverbs, too, since we use them so naturally when speaking and can use them just as naturally in writing, as Brennan-Nelson proves with this book.

She cleverly introduces each expression as a first-time listener might interpret it. For example, for "Do you have ants in your pants?" ants are depicted marching through a classroom, up a boy's legs, and into his shorts. For "The early bird gets the worm," a lunch lady is depicted serving up a big helping of "ooey, gooey, squishy worms," as children and a robin look on hungrily. By using this format, as well as providing sidebars about the origin of each expression, Brennan-Nelson invites conversations about literal meaning versus figurative meaning—and evokes a lot of laughter in the process.

I Lost My Tooth in Africa

Penda Diakité, Author
Baba Wagué Diakité, Illustrator
Scholastic, 2006

Do your students assume they're too young and inexperienced to publish a book? *I Lost My Tooth in Africa* will challenge that assumption because the author was only 8 years old when she wrote it! Inspired by a real-life incident, it is the story of Amina, a little girl with a wiggly tooth, who travels with her immediate family from Portland, Oregon, to visit her extended family in Bamako, Mali. Amina yearns to lose her tooth during the visit because, according to her father, if she places it under a calabash gourd, the African Tooth Fairy will bring her a chicken, the perfect pet. As the story unfolds, we get a fascinating glimpse into the life and language of Malian culture. We learn the words for *eggs*, *chicks*, and other commonplace things. But what we like most about this book is what the words don't say—that we are all writers, no matter how old we are.

Dear Fish

Chris Gall, Author and Illustrator
Little, Brown and Company, 2006

You've heard the old phrase "Be careful what you wish for," right? This book proves you should abide by it! One day, during a visit to the beach, young Peter Alan writes a note that he pops into a bottle and casts into the ocean: "Dear Fish, Where you live is pretty cool. You should come visit us…." Big mistake! The fish accept Peter's invitation and wreak havoc all around him. Jellyfish join a birthday party ("crashing," "smashing," "wiggling," "jiggling"). Sawfish surface at a building site ("swooping," "whooshing," "hammering," "yammering"). Octopuses occupy a beauty parlor ("combing," "curling," "snipping," "spraying"). It's pure pandemonium, captured magnificently in Gall's luminous engravings, until Peter sends another note: "Dear Fish, Thank you for coming to see us. You are nice, but you are fish. You should live at home. . . ."

A Story for Bear
Dennis Haseley, Author
Jim LaMarche, Illustrator
Harcourt, Inc., 2002

The hardest thing about writing this annotation was figuring out which chapter to put it in. We especially love the language in this book. The carefully chosen words bring the text, about a young girl and a bear, to life. The girl reads to the bear in voices to match the type of story—scary, funny, lighthearted, and so on. The bear loves the stories, is magnetized by their magic, and yearns to be able to read for himself. The ending will make you cry. This is a lovely, lovely book.

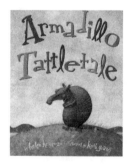

Armadillo Tattletale
Helen Ketteman, Author
Keith Graves, Illustrator
Scholastic, 2000

By definition, a tall tale stretches our imaginations because the author relies heavily on extravagant uses of words to engage the reader and create wonderful pictures of larger-than-life characters and places. Here is a tale of an armadillo that stretches the truth and learns how quickly that can get him into trouble. Much of it is clever, but all of it is excellent for word choice enthusiasts.

Rain Romp: Stomping Away a Grouchy Day
Jane Kurtz, Author
Dyanna Wolcott, Illustrator
Greenwillow Books, 2002

It's a "gray, grouchy day," and the little girl in this story would rather stay in bed than face it. But her annoyingly cheerful parents will not stand for that. Instead, they waltz around her bed, yodeling and laughing. When she can stand them no longer, the girl leaps up, dashes down the stairs, and runs outside into the pouring rain. And her frustration quickly turns to elation as she stomps about in the puddles. Soon her parents join her, and the three of them engage in a "rain romp," a wild, windswept dance celebrating their love for one another. This is a great book for teaching children about figurative language. Kurtz expertly uses simile ("Mom's and Dad's faces bob in the window like two balloons."), metaphor ("Little silver worms of rain wriggle and slither . . ."), and personification ("Dad builds a fire that . . . nibbles the middles out of sticks.").

The Night I Followed the Dog
Nina Laden, Author and Illustrator
Chronicle Books, 1994

Posing the question, "It's 10 PM . . . Do you know where your dog is?" Laden pulls off a tour de force in this book. She uses active verbs and specific nouns throughout the text and illustrates a few nouns as she goes. For example, the word *limousine* is drawn as an actual limousine with the letters inside. From the first page, you can't help but focus on the clever use of the vocabulary coupled with the ingenious presentation.

Suddenly!
Colin McNaughton, Author and Illustrator
Harcourt Brace & Company, 1995

Good word choice doesn't necessarily mean using many different words in a piece of writing. One strong word used consistently and compellingly across the piece can be just as effective. That's the case in McNaughton's side-splitting *Suddenly!* Preston the pig doesn't have a clue that a hungry wolf is stalking him. However, Preston has nothing to fear because every time the wolf is about to pounce—on the street corner, on the playground, in the grocery store—Preston "suddenly" changes direction, foiling the wolf's diabolical plan and leaving the reader to wonder who the real victim is. McNaughton cleverly uses the word "suddenly!" to indicate trouble. Each time your students hear it during read-aloud, they'll know something terrible is about to happen to the wolf, which is sure to keep them riveted to the story and rooting for Preston.

Karate Hour

Carol Nevius, Author
Bill Thomson, Illustrator
Marshall Cavendish, 2004

Whether it's cooking, gardening, or skateboarding, certain activities have a language all their own. For writers to write convincingly about an activity, they must embrace that language and use it precisely. Otherwise, readers will question their credibility. In *Karate Hour*, Nevius does a masterful job of capturing the language of karate by inviting us into a typical 60-minute class. We learn about various kinds of kicks. We learn about leaps and lunges, stances and glances. And, of course, we learn about the hierarchy of skills represented in the colored-belt system. Nevius also includes a detailed author's note on karate's history and the Japanese terminology. After reading this book aloud, have students choose a favorite activity of their own, list words associated with it, and write. Don't be surprised if their work is as rich, lyrical, and informative as Nevius's.

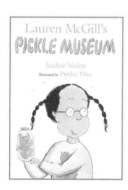

Lauren McGill's Pickle Museum

Jerdine Nolen, Author
Debbie Tilley, Illustrator
Harcourt, Inc., 2003

Lauren just loves pickles. When she goes on a class field trip and an experiment goes wrong, she saves the day—and spreads her passion for pickles to the rest of the class. This make-you-smile book delights the reader and tickles the tongue with interesting words. Powerful verbs and precise nouns and modifiers are present on every page.

Fancy Nancy

Jane O'Connor, Author
Robin Preiss Glasser, Illustrator
HarperCollins Publishers, 2006

Nancy is fancy. She likes to wear fancy clothes, eat fancy food, and, most of all, use fancy words like *chauffeur, plume*, and *merci*. However, her family is not fancy. Her mom, dad, and sister are perfectly content wearing T-shirts, eating ice-cream cones, and using ordinary words like *driver, feather*, and *thanks*. So Nancy takes it upon herself to educate them about the finer things in life by giving them a formal lesson, which ends in a wild game of dress-up. Then, to her delight, her dad suggests dinner out at the finest pizza joint in town, The King's Crown. All heads turn when Nancy and her family enter the restaurant still wearing their flamboyant getups. "They probably think we're movie stars,"

Nancy muses. But then an embarrassing incident occurs, forcing her to rethink her priorities. This is a sweet story, guaranteed to stretch your students' vocabularies.

Piggie Pie!

Margie Palatini, Author

Howard Fine, Illustrator

Houghton Mifflin Company, 1995

This is a book that will make you howl with laughter. Palatini tells the story of a bigger-than-life witch and her search for something truly delicious to eat. The hardest part of working with this book will be deciding which trait you want to focus on. We choose word choice because it is so rich in nouns, verbs, and adjectives that really work. But sentence fluency, voice, ideas, and even organization are potentials for this text, too.

These Hands

Hope Lynne Price, Author

Bryan Collier, Illustrator

Hyperion Books for Children, 1999

When you look into children's eyes, you probably see innocence, wisdom, and wonder—but mostly you see the future. In *These Hands*, Price explores that idea by looking at all the possible ways one child uses her hands—to tickle, to help, to feel, to create, to play, to pray, and, ultimately, "to sow the seeds for a brighter day." Her writing style is deceptively simple; she begins almost every sentence with the phrase "These hands. . . ." But using such a predictable language pattern allows her central idea to stand out and shine. It's a wise technique that your writers—even your most reluctant and inexperienced writers—could apply with success to their own work. And by taking their cue from the gifted Collier, your writers might also enjoy drawing pictures to illustrate each of their points.

Epossumondas

Coleen Salley, Author

Janet Stevens, Illustrator

Harcourt, Inc., 2002

You better be careful what you say because Epossumondas might bring you something you really don't want and deliver it in a way that may surprise you. Epossumondas is "the silliest, most loveable, most muddleheaded possum south of the Mason-Dixon line." This lively little story is sure to delight readers with the literal way Epossumondas carries out his sweet Auntie's directions of how to carry butter and how to hold a dog. This is the perfect book to use to teach students the importance of being accurate and precise with words.

Food Fight!
Carol Diggory Shields, Author
Doreen Gay-Kassel, Illustrator
Handprint Books, 2002

Readers will delight to find out what happens in the kitchen at night. As the food comes to life and emerges from the refrigerator, the cupboards, and the cabinets, there is a rocking good time. "'Lettuce have a party,' said the salad greens. And they slid to the floor on a bunch of string beans." A playfulness with language runs through this cute and original story—words that delight and surprise the reader.

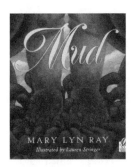

Mud
Mary Lyn Ray, Author
Lauren Stringer, Illustrator
Harcourt Brace, 2001

It takes a pretty talented author-illustrator team to transform a topic like mud into a breathtaking picture book. But that's just what Ray and Stringer have done here. Ray's text is pure poetry. She piques the reader's interest by opening with an unidentified "it": "One night it happens. Maybe it begins in the warm of day. . . . But it's always at night that it happens." That "it" is the moment the frozen earth starts melting in late winter and releases a smell "like sap in snow." From there, the earth becomes mud—squishy, squashy mud. "Happy mud," as Ray calls it. Stringer captures that description perfectly in her acrylic paintings of a child joyously stirring it, sticking it, digging it, and "dancing" it. Eventually, of course, from brown mud comes green grass. Spring arrives. This book is proof that choosing the right words can make a mundane topic magnificent.

Hello Ocean
Pam Muñoz Ryan, Author
Mark Astrella, Illustrator
Charlesbridge, 2001

Ryan is one of our favorite authors. Whether she's writing a picture book or chapter book, she takes great care, using words with skill and imagination. In this simple text, she draws on all five senses to describe the ocean. Ryan recreates all the marvelous feelings of being at the beach in language such as this: "Amber seaweed, speckled sand, bubbly waves that kiss the land" and "foggy songs from distant boats, gentle clangs from bobbing floats." Use her book as a model for sensory images in writing.

The Old Woman Who Named Things

Cynthia Rylant, Author
Kathryn Brown, Illustrator
Harcourt Brace, 1996

This is the story of an old woman who outlives all her friends and family members, and is tired of saying good-bye. So she decides to name objects that she knows will be around long after she dies. She names her car Betsy, her chair Fred, and her house Franklin. One day, a shy, brown puppy comes to her gate. The old woman gives the puppy some food and sends it away, afraid to name it for fear that it, too, will die before her. The puppy visits every day for a year but suddenly stops. Where could he be? With great relief, the old woman finds the dog at an animal shelter and brings it home. She names it Lucky, realizing that it is more important to embrace love than to fear it.

An Island Grows

Lola M. Schaefer, Author
Cathie Felstead, Illustrator
Greenwillow Books, 2006

This book does something quite remarkable: It covers centuries of geological history in only 30 pages. We see how a volcanic island forms, from the initial undersea explosion of molten lava, to the gradual buildup of solidified lava, to the arrival of plants and wildlife, and finally to the inhabitation of people. Felstead's paper collages are as beautiful as they are instructive. Schaefer's rhyming text conveys so much information in an unbelievably small number of words. No word is wasted. *An Island Grows* is one of those rare books that gives you myriad teaching points. Use it to teach about how volcanoes form. Use it teach about how communities form. Use it to teach about the power of active verbs. And use it to teach about craft—skilled writers say what they need to say by choosing each word carefully and purposefully. See focus lesson, pages 72–73.

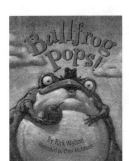

Bullfrog Pops!

Rick Walton, Author

Chris McAllister, Illustrator

Gibbs Smith, 1999

The town of Ravenous Gulch will never be the same now that Bullfrog has arrived on the scene. So hungry that he devours everything in sight, Bullfrog takes off and gets everyone he meets in an uproar as the story unfolds. What makes this book especially fun to use is that each page ends with an active verb, which prompts students to stop and predict what will come next. But the verb always leads them to a place they didn't expect, so prepare for some surprises along the way. What better way to teach students the power of active verbs than through Bullfrog's hilarious escapades?

Once There Was a Bull . . . (frog)

Rick Walton, Author

Greg Hally, Illustrator

Gibbs Smith, 1995

What's a bullfrog to do when he loses his hop? This book is about just that. Bullfrog looks everywhere for his hop! Walton teases us with his word choice. On every other page, he invites the reader to guess the last word. Examples: "He landed in a patch of grass . . ." "hoppers." and "'I'll do it,' said a cow . . ." "boy." Students have a great time predicting. Teach your students the fun of compound words with this entertaining story!

Henny-Penny

Jane Wattenberg, Author and Illustrator

Scholastic, 2000

The sky might be falling once again, but never has the event been told with more energy. Listen to this opening: "Stormy skies and whirling winds flip-flapped around the barnyard. Henny-Penny scratched about for a tasty bite to eat when . . . WHACK! An acorn smacked Henny-Penny right on top of her fine red comb." Filled with life and sparkle, this version of the familiar tale will fascinate and surprise readers . . . and inspire writers.

THREE FOCUS LESSONS ON WORD CHOICE

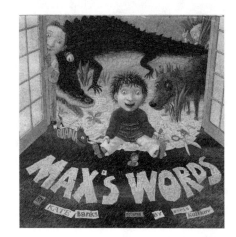

LESSON 1

Max's Words

Kate Banks, Author
Boris Kulikov, Illustrator
Farrar, Straus and Giroux, 2006

TARGET TRAIT: WORD CHOICE

Max's two older brothers have collections and Max wants one, too. So he decides to collect words—long ones, short ones, interesting ones, ones that capture his imagination. As his collection grows, he begins to organize the words into categories. Eventually, with the help of his brothers, Max writes a short story using many of his favorites. Sure to inspire young writers, this book can be used in many ways to focus on the word choice trait. In this lesson, students collect words, as Max has done, and work together to create interesting phrases and sentences.

MATERIALS:

❃ a copy of *Max's Words*

❃ small, resealable plastic containers (available at dollar stores and grocery stores)

❃ posterboard

❃ scissors

❃ glue, tape

❃ magazines, newspapers, old texts to be cut up

❃ dictionaries

❃ markers, crayons, pencils, pens

WHAT TO DO:

1. Ask students if they have any favorite words that they enjoy saying or using in their writing. Write their words on the board. Ask if they have any collections that they enjoy keeping, such as stuffed animals or trading cards.

2. Tell them you are going to read a book that has a main character who is a collector of words. Read and enjoy *Max's Words* together.

3. Discuss the story. Ask students if they might put any words from Max's list onto their list of favorite words.

4. Pass out small, resealable containers and tell students they will use them to store their own word collections. Ask them to brainstorm with you where they might find words: magazines, newspapers, greeting cards, and so on. Tell them that each time they find a word they like, they should cut it out or write it down on a slip of paper and put it in their container. They can write favorite words they find in the dictionary on slips of paper, too. Give them one week to collect all the words they want.

5. Every day, using your own collection as a model, show students how you've been adding words to your container. Be sure to collect words from a variety of sources so students see the possibilities.

6. At the end of the week, ask students to lay out all the words in their collections, read them aloud to a neighbor, and sort them as you call out the following categories:

* longest

* shortest

* funniest

* strangest

* words you hadn't heard before

* fanciest

* plainest

* hardest to say

* hardest to spell

7. Once students have categorized their words, ask them to work in groups to create interesting phrases and sentences. Tell them they can add small words such as *of, and,* and *the* to make their writing smooth.

8. Give students posterboard, scissors, and glue, and have them paste their phrases and sentences on the posterboard. Invite them to illustrate their writing to make it interesting.

9. Discuss favorite words and where students found them during their week of collecting. What was the best source? Encourage students to continue collecting words in their writer's notebook or on lists so they can use them in their writing later.

FOLLOW-UP ACTIVITIES:

* Show students how the book's illustrator, Boris Kulikov, brought the words to life by formatting them in fun ways: *Baseball* is in the shape of a bat, the *r* in *Alligator* has an eye and teeth peering out, and *Hungry* has a bite taken out of it. Invite students to illustrate their own favorite words.

* Read and enjoy *The Boy Who Loved Words* by Roni Schotter and discuss how Banks and Schotter focus on using interesting new words.

Things That Are Most in the World

Judi Barrett, Author
John Nickle, Illustrator
Atheneum Books for Young Readers, 1998

TARGET TRAIT: WORD CHOICE

Showcasing the use of superlatives, this book stretches the word choice boundaries of the reader as he or she considers how things are "most" in the world. In the lesson that follows, primary students create lively and outrageous word choice connections of their own, similar to Barrett and Nickle. As students learn about superlatives, they add a new word choice technique to their writer's bag of tricks.

MATERIALS:

❊ a copy of *Things That Are Most in the World*

❊ an overhead or chart pack

❊ paper

❊ pens, markers, crayons

WHAT TO DO:

1. Read *Things That Are Most in the World* to students, stopping and showing the pictures as you read.

2. Ask students to name favorite parts of the book and show those pages again, discussing what made them special or interesting to the student.

3. Explain that words that end with *–est* are describing words, or adjectives. They tell you something specific about a person, place, or thing. Although there are many adjectives in our language, only the ones that mean "the most," or superlatives, end in *-est*.

4. Ask students to help you make a list of adjectives and write them on the overhead. Then add *–est* to show how to make them superlatives.

> tall + est
>
> sweet + est
>
> soft + est
>
> neat + est
>
> flat + est

5. Now ask students to brainstorm a list of nouns: persons, places, and things.

> Mom or Dad
> a student
> a pet
> my room
> lunch

6. Ask students to combine one of their nouns with a superlative to form a phrase, such as "The sweetest dog in the world."

7. Ask them to take their phrase and expand it into a sentence, using the structure that Barrett uses in *Things That Are Most in the World*. "The sweetest dog in the world is the one who licks your face and snuggles up to you when your little brother is bothering you like crazy." Encourage students to use their imaginations to make their sentences interesting. Help them to get the words down, if necessary, or have them dictate their sentences to you.

8. Ask them to illustrate their sentences. Hang their creations on a bulletin board, using the title of the book as a heading: "Things That Are Most in the World."

FOLLOW-UP ACTIVITIES:

✳ Ask students to create a classroom book entitled *Things That Are Least in the World* to continue to build their word choice skills and teach them about opposites.

✳ Read and enjoy Ruth Heller's *Many Luscious Lollipops* for a different but equally delightful take on using adjectives in writing. Or, share Steve Jenkins's *Biggest, Strongest, Fastest* to give students a fine example of how superlatives are used in nonfiction writing.

LESSON 3

An Island Grows

Lola M. Schaefer, Author
Cathie Felstead, Illustrator
Greenwillow Books, 2006

TARGET TRAIT: WORD CHOICE

The power of the verb is highlighted in this superb picture book that chronicles the formation of a volcanic island. From the initial underwater eruption to the arrival of settlers, this book is punctuated with short staccato sentences: "Magma glows. / Volcano blows. / Lava flows. / An island grows." Students will select their own act of nature and write about it, using the word choice techniques of Schaefer, and create small books to share and enjoy.

MATERIALS:

❋ a copy of *An Island Grows*

❋ drawing paper

❋ pens, pencils, markers, crayons

❋ scissors

❋ glue

WHAT TO DO:

1. Read aloud *An Island Grows*.

2. Write a few sentences from the book on the whiteboard or overhead, such as "Stones break." "Water quakes." "Lava flows."

3. Put students into small groups and assign each group a sentence to act out. Ask the other students to guess the sentence after each performance.

4. Discuss the purpose of the subject and verb in each sentence. The verb contains the action. The subject is the object doing the action. Explain that verbs and subjects are essential to making sentences. Go back through the book and show students how each page contains a verb and a subject.

5. Ask students to think of other processes in nature, such as the water cycle, the life cycle of a leaf on a tree, or a hurricane.

6. Pick one process and brainstorm steps in that process with the class:

    ❋ Leaves sprout.

    ❋ Branches fill.

* Sun shines.

* Wind rustles.

* Shade soothes.

* Days shorten.

* Colors change.

* Leaves blow.

* And blow and blow.

* The tree sheds.

7. Tell students to get into pairs and to create a book about the process. Or, have them pick a different process and brainstorm steps.

8. Show students how to fold the drawing paper into book format. If you want to make an accordion book, here are some directions:

> Accordian Folded Book
> 1. Fold a 12 x 18 sheet of newsprint in half lengthwise (hot dog fold).
> 2. Open in and fold it in half widthwise (hamburger fold).
> 3. Fold it again while in the hamburger stage.
> 4. Open hamburger once.
> 5. Folded part should be positioned closest to students' body.
> 6. Cut on the middle fold going only so slightly past the next fold.
> 7. Open it back to the hot dog.
> 8. Accordion it to make a folded book. You should have about 7–8 pages to use for individual pages.
> 9. Ask students to write a sentence on each page. Have them title the book and color the cover, then illustrate the books with their own drawings or cutouts from magazines. Set the books out in the library next to *An Island Grows* for all to enjoy.

FOLLOW-UP ACTIVITIES:

* Encourage practice using subjects and verbs by having students create a schedule of activities. Each half hour, or as you change activities, ask one student to write it on the board: students pledge; math begins; reading challenges; P.E. energizes; writing relaxes; and so on. Title the schedule with a sentence students feel captures the range of what they do during the day, such as "Students Learn."

* Read aloud *Bullfrog Pops!* and point out how the author, Rick Walton, literally highlights many of the verbs in the story. Compare Schaefer's book to Walton's, one nonfiction and one fiction, and discuss how the verbs the authors use make the text lively and distinctive.

CHAPTER 5

Developing Sentence Fluency

Sentence fluency happens when writers put words and phrases together to create rhythm and flow—a melody. This is the trait that we learn by listening as much as reading. When you read these fluent picture books to students, they develop an ear for how language should sound when they try writing their own pieces. To help primary writers become fluent, we need to teach them how to do the following:

❈ begin sentences in different ways

❈ create sentences of different lengths

❈ read sentences aloud

You can show primary students how authors create fluent text by closely examining the books in this section. Note how the authors use a variety of sentence lengths and structures; point out how sentences begin. Read favorite books aloud several times. Let student marinate in the cadences and rhythms created by the authors, and encourage students to try writing passages that have similar sounds and effects.

SENTENCE FLUENCY: A DEFINITION FOR PRIMARY STUDENTS

The sentence fluency trait has two important dimensions: the grammar that makes a group of words a sentence and the way sentences sound. Indeed, this is the auditory trait, where we learn to read with our ears right along with our eyes. Signs that writers are working well with the sentence fluency trait include the following:

❋ working with several words in a row, with attention to phrasing

❋ being more concerned about sentence quality than sentence correctness

❋ experimenting with different sentences of varying lengths

❋ weaving questions and statements into the text

❋ using transitional words to connect one sentence to the next

❋ repeating sounds, words, and phrases to create a pattern

❋ writing passages that can be read aloud with ease

PICTURE BOOKS FOR DEVELOPING SENTENCE FLUENCY

Hide and Snake

Keith Baker, Author and Illustrator

Harcourt, Inc., 1991

Baker's words are simple and exact. He weaves them together seamlessly, paying careful attention to where he wants his reader to focus. Baker is a master at doing a lot with a little. In this striking work, he uses a snake to weave the message together, one simple word or phrase at a time. It's not surprising that when students choose an icon or image to stand for sentence fluency, they often pick a snake; the way the snake moves like liquid across the hard soil is a good mental image to have when writing sentences. This book uses Baker's artistry and his own well-crafted sentences to make a connection to sentence fluency.

The Important Book

Margaret Wise Brown, Author

Leonard Weisgard, Illustrator

HarperCollins, 1949

This gem has been in print for over 50 years. It features poetry that is created using a pattern, repeating the first line as the last line of the poem. In the middle, the poems are made of different numbers of nicely phrased lines. But all the poems use the same bookend strategy by beginning and ending the poem with the same line. Any time you read or write poetry, you are working with sentence fluency as you listen for the rhythm and flow of the words and phrases. After reading a few of Brown's poems, you can follow her pattern to create your own "Important Book" poems. The book is a good template for many different poem topics, such as the important thing about each of the traits, or the important thing that a student learned in school today.

Book! Book! Book!

Deborah Bruss, Author

Tiphanie Beeke, Illustrator

Scholastic, 2001

If one book will warm a picture-book lover's heart, it's this one! Summer on the farm is lovely until the children return to school and the animals find themselves bored, forlorn, and frustrated. So the horse, duck, cow, pig, goat, and hen set out on their own to find something to do—and wind up at the public library. At first, they are excited by all the happy patrons coming and going. But they become irritated when, one by one, they ask the librarian for something to do, and all she hears is "Neigh! Neigh!" "Moo! Moo!" and "Oink! Oink!" But then the hen makes her request: "Book! Book! Book!"… and the librarian finally gets it. (What librarian wouldn't, after all?!) This is a great book for teaching many things about sentence fluency, especially how to weave quotes naturally into a narrative.

Goal

Robert Burleigh, Author

Stephen T. Johnson, Illustrator

Harcourt Brace, 2001

Our eyes lit up in delight when we saw this Burleigh book at the bookstore. He never disappoints. This time his topic is the game of soccer, and as he did in his earlier piece on basketball, entitled *Hoops*, Burleigh takes us right into the center of the sport. We feel every moment through the nuances of his fluency. It would be interesting to take these two books and look at the fluency techniques he uses to make each so extraordinary. Soccer fan or not, you'll enjoy reading this. The movement Burleigh creates is masterful.

Home Run: The Story of Babe Ruth

Robert Burleigh, Author

Mike Wimmer, Illustrator

Silver Whistle, 1998

Burleigh is one of our favorite picture book authors. He has a way with words and phrases that knocks us out every time. His books' topics are always those that you know your students will love, so getting those books into their hands will be a snap. Beyond that, though, he knows how to write with beauty and grace. Listen to this excerpt from *Home Run*: "Then there is only the echoey, nothing-quite-like-it sound and the soft feel of the fat part of the bat on the center of the ball. Babe understands this feeling. He does not know when or where, but he waits for it. Again and again." Sheer poetry. What a gift this author has. When teaching sentence fluency, make sure you have at least one Robert Burleigh text!

Bat Loves the Night

Nicola Davies, Author

Sarah Fox-Davies, Illustrator

Candlewick Press, 2001

We're such fans of Davies. Her information books always strike gold. How bats live may be the subject of this book, but it is the contrasting styles of descriptive, almost poetic text and fact-focused expository text that just knocks us out.

One Tiny Turtle

Nicola Davies, Author

Jane Chapman, Illustrator

Candlewick Press, 2001

"Far, far out to sea, land is only a memory, and empty sky touches the water." Although this may sound like the opening to a great novel, it isn't. It is the opening to Davies's breathtaking *One Tiny Turtle*. Davies describes the habits and habitats of animals with remarkable clarity and compassion. In this book, we follow a loggerhead turtle as she makes her way from her nursery far out at sea to her summer and winter feeding areas and to her nesting ground—the beach where she herself was born. We experience the satisfaction of feasting on juicy crabs, clams, and shrimp; the struggle of depositing her eggs in the sand; the exhilaration of swimming from one location to another— or, as Davies puts it, "flying underwater." Nonfiction does not get better than this. See focus lesson, pages 85–87.

Rap a Tap Tap: Here's Bojangles—Think of That!

Leo Dillon and Diane Dillon, Authors and Illustrators

Blue Sky Press, 2002

Bill "Bonjangles" Robinson is arguably the greatest tap dancer of all time. But, in his lifetime, he was more than that. He was a showman, a humanitarian, and a man of the people. The Dillons capture this point magnificently in a book that overflows with rhythms and beats—so many, in fact, that it almost feels as if the words themselves are tap dancing across the page. We learn where Bill danced: on the stage, on the screen, and, most frequently, on the street. We learn for whom he danced: rich people, poor people, old people, young people, and even cats. The recurring line, "Rap a tap tap—think of that!" after each fact about Bill nudges students to contemplate his many admirable qualities, while demonstrating the effectiveness of using a single repeating sentence among a variety of other kinds of sentences.

This Jazz Man

Karen Ehrhardt, Author
R. G. Roth, Illustrator
Harcourt, Inc., 2006

Written to the tune of "This Old Man," this book will sound familiar to your students, but, chances are, everything else about it will be new to them. The men in this story are not just any old men. They are the great men of jazz—Fats Waller, Dizzy Gillespie, Duke Ellington, and Louis Armstrong, among others. Instead of playing "knickknack" on their thumbs, shoes, and knees, they play saxophone, trumpet, piano, conga, and bass to crowds of adoring fans. Roth's illustrations are as multilayered as jazz music itself, and Ehrhardt's writing quite literally sings, thanks in large part to sentences that ripple with the language of jazz. After reading the book aloud, ask students to come up with their own familiar songs, poems, or nursery rhymes and change the words to them in creative ways, as Ehrhardt does so masterfully here.

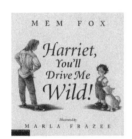

Harriet, You'll Drive Me Wild!

Mem Fox, Author
Marla Frazee, Illustrator
Harcourt, Inc., 2000

"Just like that." ". . . and she was." These two-line endings, which appear on alternating pages of this oh-so-true picture book, create a rhythm that rolls off your tongue. It is a perfectly crafted set of phrases and sentences. Fox is a master at this; her work is so satisfying to the ear. Try not to read this aloud. Go ahead, try.

Millions of Cats

Wanda Gág, Author and Illustrator
Penguin Putnam Books for Young Readers, 1928 (1996 reissue)

This classic tale of feline friendship is as delightful today as it was when it was first published in 1928. A very old man and a very old woman find themselves lonely, living in their nice clean house in the countryside. A cat is just what they need—"a sweet little fluffy cat." So the man sets out to get one, only to return with "hundreds and millions and billions and trillions" of them! This book is a classic for good reason. Its language glides and pounces with the energy of cats. Gág weaves together statements, questions, exclamations, and expressions seamlessly—and peppers them with the perfect words. She provides a superb model of a text written with great sentence fluency. See focus lesson, pages 87–88.

Farmer's Garden: Rhymes for Two Voices

David L. Harrison, Author

Arden Johnson-Petrov, Illustrator

Boyds Mills Press, 2000

In the past few years, the connection between reading fluency and reading comprehension has received a lot of attention. As a result, teachers are applying powerful oral reading strategies in their classrooms and getting impressive results. One of those strategies is choral reading of poetry, in which the whole class reads aloud a poem together or portions of the class take sections of a poem and chime in at appropriate points. *Farmer's Garden* is the perfect book for choral reading. We follow an inquisitive dog as he trots about the farm, asking the plants and animals how they grow, where they've been, what they eat, and so forth. Your students will delight in taking on the roles of the dog and his friends—and learn so much about farm life, plant and animal behavior, and, most of all, the power of a finely crafted text.

Don't Take Your Snake for a Stroll

Karin Ireland, Author

David Catrow, Illustrator

Harcourt, Inc., 2003

As every pet owner knows, there are just some places you should not go with your pet, no matter how much you love it. In this funny story, you will find out that rhinos shouldn't go dancing, pigs aren't made for shopping, and allowing chimps to hang from holiday lights leads to nothing but disaster. As you read, you and your students will find yourselves caught up in the rhythm and rhyme of each page. Encourage students to try Ireland's pattern in their own writing. Let them think of other animals and places where they wouldn't take them because of their natural behaviors and physical characteristics.

Bad Dog

Nina Laden, Author and Illustrator

Walker & Company, 2000

Without a doubt, this book is a perfect fit for word choice and sentence fluency. But because we have listed a couple of other Laden books under word choice, let's look at this one a bit differently. This book has great sentences—flashy and brilliant with that "just right" feel. Laden begins, "So they say I'm a bad dog. I know I'm no Saint Bernard, but it's not like I robbed a bank or anything." She moves on to "I was bored. Running on empty. Empty water dish, empty food bowl. So I emptied the trash can. That's when I found it. My inspiration." The careful combination of chopped phrases and long sentences makes this book a good one to study for sentence fluency.

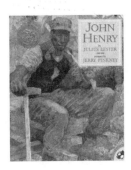

John Henry

Julius Lester, Author

Jerry Pinkney, Illustrator

Puffin Books, 1994

This retelling of the classic heroic tale of the human spirit contains powerful imagery and carefully chosen words and phrases, making it a fine piece to examine for sentence fluency. You'll also love it for its humor and compassion. Try reading this version to students and then reading another author's version. Which one is stronger in each of the traits? Lester's version scores high on sentence fluency, word choice, and voice.

The Web Files

Margie Palatini, Author

Richard Egielski, Illustrator

Hyperion Books, 2001

This book screams sentence fluency and word choice. From the line "Someone has pilfered a peck of perfect purple almost-pickled peppers," we are sent on a captivating, mystery-solving adventure. But it's not only the language choices that make this piece stand out. Ellipses, hyphens, dashes, and a full range of other punctuation marks draw you into the text and create the energy and flow of the work. The story is written in a detective genre style: the facts, ma'am, nothing but the facts. Short, chopped sentences with alliteration to tie your tongue over make this a favorite text.

Poetry Speaks to Children

Elise Paschen, Editor

Billy Collins, Nikki Giovanni, and X. J. Kennedy, Advisory Editors

Judy Love, Wendy Rasmussen, and Paula Zinngrabe Wendland, Illustrators

Sourcebooks, Inc., 2005

Poetry Speaks to Children is a smorgasbord of the finest poems by the finest poets of all time—from William Shakespeare to Janet S. Wong. The editors, many of them exceptional poets in their own right, have gone to great lengths to ensure the 95 lavishly illustrated poems represent a range of races, religions, and genders. Some of the poems are witty, such as Maxine Kumin's "Sneeze," some are whimsical, such as John Ciardi's "About the Teeth of Sharks," and some are profound, such as Langston Hughes's "The Negro Speaks of Rivers." What they share, though, is magnificent language. As a bonus, the book comes with a CD of 52 of the poems, many read by the poets who wrote them, making *Poetry Speaks to Children* invaluable for teaching about sentence fluency.

Canoe Days

Gary Paulsen, Author
Ruth Wright Paulsen, Illustrator
Doubleday Books for Young Readers, 1999

Like so many Paulsen-Paulsen collaborations, this book takes a simple idea—canoeing on a lake—and elevates it to nothing short of epic. The book opens with a rower dropping his boat into the water, picking up his paddle, and setting out into "water so quiet it becomes part of the sky." As he glides along, he witnesses an active world that belies the tranquility of the day: "a snake moves from shore to pad, a wavy ripple…" "a fox drinks, soft laps with a pink tongue…" "a mallard hen, her ducklings spread out like a spotted fan around her…." Because of lovely observations like these, brought to life by Ruth Wright Paulsen's stunning illustrations, the reader leaves the book feeling as spiritually moved as the rower himself. This book is about much more than canoeing. It is about communing with nature—and honoring and maintaining our relationship to it.

Dogteam

Gary Paulsen, Author
Ruth Wright Paulsen, Illustrator
Delacorte Press, 1995

Close your eyes and try to imagine the feeling of driving a dogsled on a cold, crisp, clear night. Gary Paulsen recreates this image through the rhythm and cadence of his writing. "Through the trees, in and out, the sled whipping after them, through the trees with no sound but the song of the runners, the high-soft-shusshh-whine of the runners." When students hear this book read aloud, they will feel themselves being whisked through the snow right along with the author.

Charlie Parker Played Be Bop

Chris Raschka, Author and Illustrator
Orchard Press, 1992

One of the best ways to determine whether students understand the rules of standard English is to see whether they can break those rules wisely and with purpose, as Raschka does so well in this homage to legendary jazz musician Charlie

Parker. Raschka whips up a way-out combination of complete sentences that inform—"Charlie Parker played saxophone"—and sentence fragments that capture the sound of be bop—"Bobbity, bibbitty, bop. Bang!" As a result, students get a clear sense of the man and his music, without actually hearing a note. While reading this book aloud, don't be surprised if students chime in, unprompted. The cool beats and rhythms are contagious—and Raschka's illustrations jump from the page as forcefully as Parker's melodies jump from the horn.

Two Cool Cows
Toby Speed, Author
Barry Root, Illustrator
Putnam, 1995

One look at this book's whimsical cover of two cool cows, complete with shades, and you'll know you are in for a romp. The cows swing through familiar nursery rhymes with energy and bounce, never missing a beat. The text reads like free verse poetry in some places, rhyming text in others, and has tons of terrific tongue twisters.

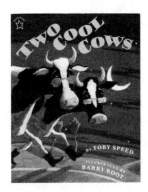

The Dragon Machine
Helen Ward, Author
Wayne Anderson, Illustrator
Dutton Children's Books, 2003

Young George has quite a problem: Dragons are following him everywhere—dragons that are as "ignored and overlooked" as George himself is. Initially, he enjoys the chubby, scaly, spear-tailed beasts, watching them chase butterflies, tease cats, and eat stale cookies and stinky cheese. But eventually they get on his nerves. So George builds a flying machine to lure them to a far-off land where dragons roam freely. Everything is going according to plan, until a crash landing prevents George from returning home. His parents rescue him and, in the process, truly recognize him for the first time in his life. This is a lovely story containing sentences that not only stand strong in isolation, but also flow into one another seamlessly.

A Chair for My Mother
Vera B. Williams, Author and Illustrator
Greenwillow Books, 1982

There are many things we admire about this Caldecott Honor book: its delightfully primitive illustrations, its straightforward structure that incorporates a flashback. But what we like most is its plot. It's a great story, plain and simple. A little girl, her mother, and grandmother save coins in a jar to buy a chair—"a wonderful, beautiful, fat, soft armchair"—after all their furniture is lost in a fire. As the title makes clear, the chair is for the mother who works in a diner and needs a comfortable spot to rest when she returns home each evening. Told from the perspective of the little girl, the story demonstrates just how fluent writing can be when the writer focuses on the natural rhythms of spoken language. Read this book to your students and then ask them to write their own first-person stories, thinking about how it sounds as well as what it says. See focus lesson, pages 89–90.

The Seashore Book

Charlotte Zolotow, Author
Wendell Minor, Illustrator
HarperCollins Publishers, 1992

A little boy from the mountains longs to learn about the seashore, so his mother plays a game of pretend with him. She describes, in the most visual way possible, the arc of day by the ocean. Through her words alone, the little boy imagines the sights and sounds of the seashore. He is there, and so is the reader. The sentences in this book rise and fall as effortlessly as the surf itself. Zolotow stirs up a salty blend of figurative language, dialogue, expressions, questions, simple and complex sentences. As a fun post-reading activity, ask your students to describe in writing something that they have experienced but their reader hasn't—maybe sledding on a snow-covered hill, walking the streets of New York City, or celebrating a holiday such as Passover or Ramadan.

THREE FOCUS LESSONS ON SENTENCE FLUENCY

LESSON 1

One Tiny Turtle

Nicola Davies, Author
Jane Chapman, Illustrator
Candlewick Press, 2001

TARGET TRAIT: SENTENCE FLUENCY

In this stunning picture book, Davies uses fluid, descriptive language to explain the life cycle of loggerhead sea turtles. And, like in her books on whales, bats, and polar bears, she drops in "factlets," interesting, well-researched bits of information throughout, providing the reader with yet another way of interacting with her beautifully written text. In this lesson, while listening to *One Tiny Turtle* read aloud, students determine whether sentences are complete or fragments. Then they use this understanding to create captions for pictures in which they describe what they learn about loggerhead sea turtles.

MATERIALS:

❊ a copy of *One Tiny Turtle*

❊ paper

❊ pens, pencils, markers, crayons

❊ chart paper

WHAT TO DO:

1. Ask students if they have ever heard of loggerhead sea turtles and, if so, to explain what they know.

2. Tell them you are going to read a book about loggerhead sea turtles and, as you read, you'd like them to not only listen for fascinating pieces of information, but also for the author's sentence fluency—how she makes the text easy to listen to.

3. Read the book, pausing to show the pictures as you go. When you come to a page that has informational notes, or "factlets," show students how the author sets factlets apart from the running text. Ask them if they hear any difference in the sentence fluency of factlets versus the running text.

4. Explain to students that complete sentences have a subject and a verb (a doer and an action). Fragments are only parts of sentences. Tell students that writers use complete sentences most often, but occasionally they use a fragment to change the way a passage sounds. Fragments can change the rhythm and tempo of the writing to make it pleasing to the ear. They can also be used to make important ideas stand out in the text.

5. Tell students you are going to reread some sentences from the book, and they are going to determine whether they are complete or not by listening to them carefully.

6. Read the following sentences aloud to the students. Tell them to put their thumb up if they think a sentence is complete and down if they think it is not. If you wish, make an overhead to show the correct answer after they've made their decisions.

   - She's a baby, so her shell is soft as old leather. (thumb up)
   - Safe in her world of weed. (thumb down)
   - Fish breathe underwater, but turtles are reptiles. (thumb up)
   - She pokes her pinprick nostrils through the silver surface to take a quick breath, so fast, blink and you'd miss it! (thumb up)
   - When you look for her. (thumb down)
   - Rides out the storm. (thumb down)
   - Her head is tough as a helmet. (thumb up)
   - A glimpse of her. (thumb down)
   - Left behind, under the sand, her eggs stay deep and safe. (thumb up)
   - And before the summer's over they wriggle from their shells. (thumb up)
   - Swims and swims! (thumb down)
   - One day, she'll remember this beach and come back. (thumb up)

7. Tell students they are going to try writing complete and incomplete sentences of their own. Ask them to recall a fact about loggerhead turtles from the text and write it out in a complete sentence.

8. Ask students to draw a picture to go along with their sentence and write a short caption underneath it that is a fragment.

9. Compare the two pieces of writing, pointing out for students what makes one a complete sentence and the other not. Discuss how students can use fragments in their writing to change how the fluency sounds to the reader.

Follow-Up Activities:

- During the discussion of the book, students most likely had questions about loggerhead sea turtles that the book couldn't answer. Help them to write those questions out and use the Internet to find answers. Then, write the questions and answers on chart paper for all to see. Use complete sentences for the questions, and fragments for the answers explaining that writers do this all the time when they want to fit a lot of information into a small space.

❊ Read and enjoy other books by this remarkable author, such as *Bat Loves the Night; Extreme Animals; White Owl, Barn Owl; Ice Bear; Big Blue Whale;* and *Surprising Sharks*. You and your students will delight in how beautifully Davies writes, and how fascinating she makes each animal.

LESSON 2

Millions of Cats

Wanda Gág, Author and Illustrator
Penguin Putnam Books for Young Readers, 1928
(1996 reissue)

TARGET TRAIT: SENTENCE FLUENCY

Few stories stand up to the test of time, and this is one of them. From the minute you read its familiar refrain, "Cats here, cats there, cats and kittens everywhere. Hundreds of cats, thousands of cats, millions and billions and trillions of cats!" you are taken back to your own childhood and a time when this book earned its spot among your most favorite. It certainly was at the top of our list along with *Ferdinand the Bull* and *Make Way for Ducklings*. Your students will enjoy a choral reading of this fluent text and then writing and illustrating a favorite line to share with the group.

MATERIALS:

❊ a copy of *Millions of Cats*

❊ paper

❊ pencils, pens, markers in black, red, and white

❊ tape

WHAT TO DO:

1. Tell students that you are going to read them a story that they may have heard at home or in another class. It's a classic. Explain what a classic is.

2. Read the story, emphasizing the repeating lines.

3. Ask students what they liked about the story. Tell them that you're going to read the book again but this time they are going to read parts right along with you.

4. Divide the class into two groups. Tell the first group that, when you point at it, its members will say— "Cats, here . . ." Tell the second group to join in with "cats there . . ." when you point to it. Tell the whole group to say "cats and kittens everywhere" when you give them the cue.

5. Give the next line to the first group, "Hundreds of cats. . . ." Give the line after that to the second group, "Thousands of cats…" and have everyone chant in unison, "millions and billions and trillions of cats!"

6. Practice the choral reading part of the story until the two groups have their parts down fully.

7. Read the whole story again from beginning to end, stopping to let each group recite its lines. Cue them if necessary.

8. When finished, ask students to tell you if they thought Gág's writing had rhythm and flowed smoothly.

9. Ask students to pick their favorite line and write it out. Then ask students to draw a picture of their favorite line on a separate paper. Encourage them to match Gág's style of Russian woodcuts using black, red, and white.

10. Put the pictures up around the room and ask students to read their line aloud one at a time, prompting classmates to guess which picture it matches. When a match is made, tape the sentence to its picture.

11. Note which lines, if any, were selected by more than one student. Ask students to explain why more people liked those lines than the others.

FOLLOW-UP ACTIVITIES:

✤ Sometimes authors create rhyming schemes to make the text flow easily and musically. Re-examine *Million of Cats* with students for the use of rhyme as one of the techniques Gág uses to create fluent prose.

✤ Share Mem Fox's book *Koala Lou* and point out how Fox, like Gág, also uses a repeating refrain throughout, "Koala Lou, I do love you."

LESSON 3

A Chair for My Mother

Vera B. Williams, Author and Illustrator
Greenwillow Books, 1982

TARGET TRAIT: SENTENCE FLUENCY

When a fire destroys everything they own, Rosa and her family save all their pennies until they can buy a new chair for her mother—a chair where she can rest after working all day at a diner, and where the family can gather. This is a remarkably well-written book largely because Williams varies the structure and length of her sentences to achieve fluency. In this lesson, students "dissect" her sentences by putting mixed-up words in order and noting how the sentences begin. At the end, students will write a new sentence of their own, making sure to begin it differently than those from the book.

MATERIALS:

❊ a copy of *A Chair for My Mother*

❊ writing paper

❊ pencils and pens

❊ sentences from the book:

1. We set the chair right beside the window with the red and white curtains.
2. Grandma and Mama and I all sat in it while Aunt Ida took our picture.
3. Now Grandma sits in it and talks with people going by in the daytime.
4. Mama sits down and watches the news on TV when she comes home from her job.
5. After supper, I sit with her and she can reach right up and turn out the light if I fall asleep in her lap.

    ❊ copy and cut apart, word by word

    ❊ put each set of words in a separate envelope

    ❊ number the outside of each envelope 1–5

WHAT TO DO:

1. Ask students to talk about their favorite possessions and how much they appreciate having them.

---

2. Tell them that the main characters in the story you are going to read lose all their favorite possessions in a fire.

3. Encourage students to talk about ways they could help someone who experiences such a tragedy. Could they donate some of their toys and things to children who lose theirs? Could they and their families collect money to donate to other families? Could they volunteer at places such as the local food bank?

4. Read aloud *A Chair for My Mother* and discuss how the family saves money to buy a new chair.

5. Tell students that one way an author works to make a story as good as this one is to write the sentences very carefully. Tell them that you have prepared an activity for them to learn this firsthand by recreating the sentences from *A Chair for My Mother*.

6. Organize the class into small groups, and give each group an envelope containing words from sentences in the book. Tell students to put all the words out on their table and organize them in a way that creates sentences that sound correct. Encourage them to read their sentences aloud, listening for phrases that work well together.

7. Allow time to work. When each group has finished, ask members to write down the first two words of their sentence on a piece of paper and label them with the number written on the envelope. For example, Sentence # 1: "It was." Then ask students to put the words back in the envelope and trade envelopes with another group.

8. Continue this process until the groups have configured and documented all five. All groups should have a list of all five sentence beginnings.

9. Ask students which sentence was the hardest to put back in order and which was the easiest. Then ask students to look at their lists and tell you what they notice. They should comment that no two sentences began the same way. If they don't, point that fact out to them. Explain why sentence variety is key to the trait of sentence fluency.

10. Ask students to write one new sentence for the book, a sentence that comes at the end. This sentence should explain the object that Rosa would like to save up for and replace next. It should not begin "After supper" since the sentence before it begins that way.

11. Share the sentences. Discuss.

FOLLOW-UP ACTIVITIES:

❖ Ask students to draw pictures of the object that they pick for Rosa to buy and write their sentences under the pictures. Hang the creations so everyone can see and then decide which object would be the best one to replace next.

❖ Read *Saving Strawberry Farm* by Deborah Hopkinson, another fine book about prioritizing and saving money.

CHAPTER 6

Strengthening
Conventions

onventions should guide the reader through the text, making it easy to read and understand. We use standard conventions in English so readers don't fail to engage with the ideas because of poor spelling or missing punctuation. We can help primary writers learn to use conventions with confidence by encouraging them to do the following:

❋ learn how to spell words that matter

❋ practice accurate capitalization

❋ use punctuation to enhance meaning

Primary writers who learn the basics of conventions understand how important they are to the reader. By showing students how published authors use conventions in these books, you invite students to acknowledge the role of conventions in the best writing, and give them examples of how conventions should look in their own pieces.

CONVENTIONS: A DEFINITION FOR PRIMARY STUDENTS

Primary writers are too young and inexperienced to show control over sophisticated conventions, but there are certain ones they can follow to make their writing correct and understandable, including using the following:

❊ imitation and real letters

❊ upper- and lowercase letters

❊ conventional spelling of simple words

❊ phonetic spelling of both simple and sophisticated words

❊ end punctuation

❊ capital letters at the beginning of sentences, on proper nouns, and in titles

❊ *s* for plurals and possessives

❊ contractions

❊ indented paragraphs

PICTURE BOOKS FOR STRENGTHENING CONVENTIONS

Our Librarian Won't Tell Us ANYTHING!
Toni Buzzeo, Author
Sachiko Yoshikawa, Illustrator
Upstart Books, 2006

You've heard the old proverb about fishing "Give a man a fish and you feed him for a day. Teach a man to fish and you feed him for a lifetime," right? Well, the same rule applies to using the library, as this book proves. Fourth grader Carmen is convinced that librarian Mrs. Skorupski is the most unhelpful grown-up at Liberty Elementary School because she won't give her what she asks for. But when Carmen is paired up with Robert, "The Library Success Story," to carry out a predator-prey project, things change. Mrs. Skorupski gives Carmen the tools to find the information she needs—and her collaboration with Robert blossoms. This book holds many lessons, including using all capitals to emphasize key words. Buzzeo uses this technique in the title and carries it through the entire book.

Captain's Purr

Madeleine Floyd, Author and Illustrator

Harcourt, Inc., 2003

With its simple sentences and sentence patterns, this story of a cat and his everyday activities conjures up memories of the Dick and Jane series—"Here is Captain, our very handsome cat. We love Captain. Captain likes to sleep. He sleeps on my bed…." But don't let Floyd's unadorned writing style discourage you from using her book as a model for all the traits, especially conventions. She has created a believable and adorable character in Captain, organized the story in a sensible way (morning to night), chosen her words carefully, included an unexpected plot twist that will delight your students, and, yes, used conventions with utmost precision and clarity. It's all here, waiting for your students to emulate in their own writing.

Beatrice Doesn't Want To

Laura Numeroff, Author

Lynn Munsinger, Illustrator

Candlewick Press, 2004

From the author of *If You Give a Mouse a Cookie* comes this equally charming book about Henry, a boy who has a report to do at the library, and his book-despising little sister, Beatrice, who doesn't want to join him. But she must join him because, much to his misery, Henry's in charge of her. During two trips to the library, Beatrice does nothing but whine, whimper, and pester poor Henry. But on the third trip, the librarian's read-aloud takes hold of her imagination and changes her mind about books forever. *Beatrice Doesn't Want To* is guaranteed to take hold of your students with its spot-on characterizations of the overburdened big brother and the self-centered little sister. Once you have them, read the book again for conventions. Numeroff's uncomplicated but carefully crafted prose is sure to enlighten any young writer.

Tulip Sees America

Cynthia Rylant, Author

Lisa Desimini, Illustrator

Blue Sky Press, 1998

This is the story of a bad case of wanderlust. As a boy growing up in Ohio, the narrator never went anywhere because his parents were homebodies. So, as a young man, he hits the road in a green VW Beetle with his dog, Tulip. Popular tourist attractions don't interest him, though. Natural wonders do. He visits the skies of Nebraska, the wind of Wyoming, the mountains of Colorado, and the desert of Nevada, and finally he makes a home for himself and Tulip by the ocean in Oregon. Whether you use this book to teach something as sophisticated as choosing small details to make a big point or something as basic as beginning the names of states with a capital letter, you won't be sorry. Like so many of Rylant's books, *Tulip Sees America* delivers on many levels.

Duck on a Bike

David Shannon, Author and Illustrator

Scholastic, 2002

Shannon loves to write about being naughty. *No, David!, Alice the Fairy,* and this book—the story of a mischievous duck that flaunts his bicycle-riding skills before all his barnyard friends—prove it. And, let's face it, kids love being naughty sometimes, which is precisely why they love Shannon's books so much. This book is particularly good for teaching about conventions because its undemanding yet thoroughly entertaining plot allows you to focus on many, many good examples of standard rules in use: using quotation marks, using a variety of end punctuation marks, and capitalizing proper names. You can easily pull passages, explore them with the class, and have students apply what they learn to their own work. See focus lesson, on pages 97–99.

So You Want to Be President?

Judith St. George, Author

David Small, Illustrator

Penguin Putnam Books for Young Readers, 2000

With so little time in the school day, we need to choose books that give us the biggest educational bang for our buck, as *So You Want to Be President?* does. Not only does it serve as a great model for using capital letters at the beginning of people's names, it contains a ton of information about past commanders in chief. For example, did you know Taft was the heaviest president and had a special bathtub built to accommodate his large frame? Or Coolidge had a pet raccoon? Or Nixon played the piano? Or Andrew Johnson didn't learn to write until well into his adulthood? But what our past presidents share, as St. George points out so eloquently, is that they were all natural leaders, patriots, and, most of all, human beings, just like the rest of us.

Where Are You Going? To See My Friend!

Eric Carle and Kazuo Iwamura, Authors and Illustrators

Scholastic, 2001

Two giants of children's literature come together to tell a story that crosses languages, cultures, and artistic styles. One by one, a dog, cat, rooster, goat, and rabbit meet up on a journey that culminates in high-spirited singing and dancing. The first half of the book is written in English and illustrated in collage by Carle. It is loaded with dialogue that serves as a wonderful model for your young writers. The second half is the same story, written in Japanese and illustrated in watercolor by Iwamura. This is also a terrific book for teaching about presentation—specifically, showing students how two illustrators can use very different techniques to tell the same story.

The Great Fuzz Frenzy

Janet Stevens and Susan Stevens Crummel, Authors

Janet Stevens, Illustrator

Harcourt, Inc., 2005

Life in the prairie-dog hole is peaceful until, out of nowhere, a big, round object falls from the sky—a tennis ball, actually—and creates chaos. At first, the hole's chubby, buck-toothed inhabitants are apprehensive, but once they realize that the object will cause them no harm, they begin plucking green fuzz from it and fashioning it into scarves, capes, tutus, and other accessories. When the ball is plucked bald, however, and the fuzz fortune dries up, there's all-out war. That's when Big Bark, the leader, steps in to wage peace, only to be cast into peril himself, forcing the other prairie dogs to band together to rescue him. This book is a natural read-aloud. Your students will not only love the story, but also learn a thing or two about formatting quotes because the story is told almost entirely in dialogue.

When I Am Old With You

Angela Johnson, Author

David Soman, Illustrator

Orchard Books, 1990

When it comes to writing, punctuation is often associated with standards of correctness. And adhering to such standards is important. But crafting a piece of writing—looking closely at *what* it says and *how* it says it—is equally important. Punctuation can help us do that. In *When I Am Old With You*, for example, Johnson uses commas to emphasize an influential person in the narrator's life: "In the mornings, Grandaddy, we will cook bacon for breakfast and that's all." She uses ellipses to emphasize a moment of thought: "It might make us cry . . . but that's O.K." She uses a recurring contraction to emphasize the bond between the narrator and his grandfather: "We'll go fishing . . . ," We'll play cards . . . ," "We'll drink cool water from a jug . . . ." These are intentional moves—moves worth teaching to help your students use punctuation as a craft tool.

Eats, Shoots & Leaves: Why, Commas Really Do Make a Difference!
Lynne Truss, Author
Bonnie Timmons, Illustrator
G. P. Putnam's Sons, 2006

Are you one of those people who think a misused comma every now and then is no big deal? If so, you won't feel that way after reading this book. Truss makes a compelling argument for using the comma in all the right places—or risk real embarrassment as a writer. For example, "Look at the huge, hot dog" means something entirely different from "Look at the huge hot dog." The former is telling the reader to notice a gigantic parched pooch, whereas the latter is telling him or her to notice a gigantic wiener. Like we said, embarrassing! *Eats, Shoots & Leaves* is loaded with hilarious comparisons like these, brought to life by Timmons's witty, whimsical illustrations. You'll have a field day sharing them with your students and talking about how one tiny comma can change meaning in big ways.

Alexander and the Terrible, Horrible, No Good, Very Bad Day
Judith Viorst, Author
Ray Cruz, Illustrator
Atheneum, 1972

You needn't look further than this book's title to learn something about commas—but please do, because it's wonderful. A contemporary classic! Alexander has a feeling he's in for a bad day when he wakes up with gum in his hair, and he's right. Things just spiral downward from there. At breakfast, his two brothers find prizes in their cereal boxes, but Alexander doesn't. At school, his classmate Paul receives praise for his picture, but Alexander doesn't. In the car, all the other kids get window seats, but Alexander doesn't. What does Alexander get? A cavity, lima beans, and soap in his eyes. Talk about a bad day! Read the book once for the sole purpose of enjoying the story. Then read it again, pointing out all the places Viorst uses the serial comma. Learning about punctuation was never this fun.

Don't Let the Pigeon Drive the Bus!
Mo Willems, Author and Illustrator
Hyperion Books for Children, 2003

If you haven't shared Willems's books with your students, buckle your seatbelt. You're in for a wild ride! The story here couldn't be simpler: On the first page, a bus driver announces to readers he's got to step away and implores, "Don't let the pigeon drive the bus!" And the moment he leaves, who shows up? You guessed it—the pigeon, who spends the remainder of the book trying to convince readers to let him take the wheel. "I'll be careful." "What's the big deal?" "I never get to do anything!" When reading this book silently, we can practically hear the joyful voices of children, responding "no, no, no…" to the pigeon's every plea. As a bonus, Willems uses every conceivable form of end punctuation—periods, question marks, quotation marks, exclamation points—in sentences that are easy to extract and examine as a group. Whatever you do, don't let this book pass you by!

A FOCUS LESSON ON CONVENTIONS

Duck on a Bike
David Shannon, Author and Illustrator
Scholastic, 2002

Whimsical and zany, this fun-filled mentor text is wonderful for showing students how capital letters can be used to make important words stand out. Duck, who is a little bit on the wild and crazy side anyway, takes a ride around the farm on a red bike, causing quite the ruckus among the other animals who are convinced that Duck has lost his mind. As they converse about Duck's latest antics, readers will notice strategically used capital letters making certain lines emphatic. In this lesson, students learn how capitals are used for proper nouns. They also learn about articles and practice using capital letters by turning common nouns into proper nouns.

MATERIALS:

❄ a copy of *Duck on a Bike*

❄ paper

❄ pencils, pens

❄ overhead transparency of text from the last page of the book

WHAT TO DO:

1. Ask students to write their first name on a piece of paper, capitalizing the first letter. Then ask them to write a descriptor of some sort next to the name: a boy, a girl, a student, a friend, a soccer player, a pizza-eater, for example. Point out that they do not capitalize the descriptor, only their actual name.

2. Explain the difference between a proper noun (a specific person, place, or thing) and a common noun (a generic person, place, or thing). Remind them to capitalize proper nouns, but not common ones unless they come at the beginning of a sentence.

3. Tell them that you are going to read a book that uses common nouns as names and shows how the author makes this clear by using capitalization.

4. Read *Duck on a Bike*, pausing to show pages where *Duck* is capitalized because it's his name, not just his species. Do the same for Dog, Cat, Horse, Chicken, Goat, Pig and Pig, and Mouse.

5. On the overhead show the text from the last page.

> "Then they put the bikes back by the house. And no one
> knew that on that afternoon, there had been a cow, a sheep,
> a dog, a cat, a horse, a chicken, a goat, two pigs, a mouse,
> and a duck on a bike."

6. Ask students why the author did not capitalize the names of the animals on this page. See if they notice that the article *a* or a number in front of the animal name signals a common noun. Tell students that, typically, three articles signal a common noun is coming: *a, an, the*.

7. Once they grasp this concept, ask students to rewrite the last page to make the animal names into proper nouns. It should read like this:

> "Then they put the bikes back by the house. And no one
> knew that on that afternoon, there had been Cow, Sheep,
> Dog, Cat, Horse, Chicken, Goat, Pig and Pig, Mouse, and
> Duck on a bike."

FOLLOW-UP ACTIVITIES:

❊ Ask students to write the beginning to a story, using proper nouns as Shannon does in *Duck on a Bike*. *A mother* would change to *Mother*; *a child* would change to *Child*; *a dog* would change to *Dog*. Encourage them have some fun experimenting with proper and common nouns.

❊ Read the book *My Duck* by Tanya Linch, pointing out how frequently the term *my duck* is used. Copy two pages from the text that contain *my duck*, and ask students to read them with you and change *my duck* to the proper noun, *Duck*. Now ask students to help read the rest of the book with you, replacing *my duck* with *Duck*. Ask students if they found any other terms in the book that could be changed to a proper noun, such as *my teacher*.

CHAPTER 7

Spotlighting
Presentation

Appearance, or the visual appeal of the pictures and words to readers, are at the heart of this trait. When the writer has finally captured everything he or she wants to say, then it is time to consider how to put the words and pictures together to make it appealing to the reader. Primary students can learn to work successfully with presentation when we teach them to do the following:

❉ space letters, words, and sentences wisely

❉ use their best handwriting

❉ draw carefully

These books were selected because they show strength in presentation. Whether it is through the interesting use of white space, the choice of font, the style of the illustrations, or how the text and pictures are laid out on the page, each book has visual appeal. Invite students to note the elements they think make text the most appealing and try those techniques in pieces of their own.

PRESENTATION: A DEFINITION FOR PRIMARY STUDENTS

Presentation relates to how the writing appears on the paper. It's often a measure of how much care students have put into their work. If they have spent a lot of time drafting, revising, and editing, they usually want the final product to look good. They want to publish and share it. You and they may both check for the following:

❁ margins that frame the writing and pictures

❁ carefully formed letters

❁ neat, legible printing

❁ letters and words that stay on the lines

❁ clearly laid out pictures and text

❁ carefully drawn pictures

❁ appropriate and simple use of fonts if the child is using a computer

❁ a finished, polished piece of writing with no or few cross-outs or smudges

PICTURE BOOKS FOR SPOTLIGHTING PRESENTATION

I Will Never Not Ever Eat a Tomato

Lauren Child, Author and Illustrator
Candlewick Press, 2000

Calling Lola a picky eater is an understatement. She's a defiant eater. She detests carrots because they're for rabbits, peas because they're too small and green, and almost all other foods—potatoes, fish sticks, and especially tomatoes—for reasons she doesn't disclose. She just hates them. That is, until her brother Charlie begins playing a mind game that convinces Lola the carrots are not carrots, but "orange twiglets from Jupiter." The peas are "green drops from Greenland." The potatoes are "cloud fluffs from Mount Fuji." The fish sticks are "ocean nibbles." By the time Lola and Charlie move on to tomatoes, she's onto his game, and names them herself: "moonsquirters." This book is a wild amalgam of media: drawings, photographs, and even fabric and wallpaper swatches, with type winding in and around the illustrations blissfully.

The Story of Frog Belly Rat Bone

Timothy Basil Ering, Author and Illustrator
Candlewick Press, 2003

In grim, gray Cementland lives a boy who dreams of finding a treasure. One day, his dream is realized when he discovers a box with a note attached that reads, "Put my wondrous riches into the earth and enjoy." Inside the box are packages of "tiny gray specks," and the boy plants some of the specks, as instructed. Before anything happens to them, though, a crafty rat, rabbit, and fruit fly exhume and steal them one night. To prevent future thefts, the boy creates a monster to guard his treasure, and it works. In fact, it works so well, the boy, monster, rat, rabbit, and fruit fly become friends and, as a team, transform Cementland into a virtual Shangri-La. Ering's handwritten text, luminescent paintings, and creepy yet somehow cuddly characters are sure to grab your students' attention and teach them an important lesson in presentation.

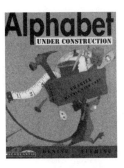

Alphabet Under Construction

Denise Fleming, Author and Illustrator
Henry Holt and Company, 2002

If you're like most primary teachers, teaching letters and letter sounds is a high priority. But finding good materials—materials other than flashcards, alphabet friezes, and canned programs—can be a challenge. That is, until you check out the children's section of your library or bookstore. There are tons of excellent alphabet books available today, including this one by Fleming, in which a very busy, buck-toothed mouse "measures," "saws," "nails," and carries out 23 other tasks to construct each letter of the alphabet. Fleming pours colored cotton fiber through hand-cut stencils to create her illustrations—bright, bold renderings that will burst from the page during read-aloud. Don't be surprised if your students want to try their hands at constructing alphabet books after enjoying this one.

Giant Pandas

Gail Gibbons, Author and Illustrator

Holiday House, Inc., 2002

It never ceases to amaze us just how much information Gibbons fits into a 32-page picture book. Whether she's writing about pumpkins, planets, or penguins, she covers all the bases, in a voice that parallels great fiction more than traditional nonfiction. *Giant Pandas* is no exception. From page 1, we learn about where the panda lives, what it eats, how it procreates, how it enjoys itself, how it defends itself, and the forces that threaten its existence. Gibbons uses a variety of visual elements—labels, diagrams, call-outs, maps—to reinforce the points she makes in the text. Read this book in its entirety to the class and then focus on specific elements, encouraging students to use those elements in their own writing. You should see amazing strides in their presentation.

Ben's Trumpet

Rachel Isadora, Author and Illustrator

Greenwillow Books, 1979

Ben is a little boy growing up in the big city during the 1920s. What he enjoys more than anything is sitting on the fire escape on steamy summer nights, playing his imaginary trumpet to the music drifting from the Zig Zag Jazz Club right nearby. But as happy as playing his imaginary trumpet makes him, he longs for a real one so that one day he can accompany his heroes inside the club—the pianist, the saxophonist, the trombonist, the drummer, and especially the trumpet player. Isadora's black-and-white illustrations are pure magic, capturing the art deco style of the day. They prove you don't need color to create a striking, Caldecott-caliber presentation.

Biggest, Strongest, Fastest

Steve Jenkins, Author and Illustrator

Houghton Mifflin Company, 1995

The idea here is so brilliantly simple, it's amazing no creator of picture books had thought of it sooner: Gather together all animals that hold the record for various qualities—biggest, strongest, fastest, and so forth. Jenkins uses his canvas to its fullest. For example, he shows a blue whale, the largest animal, bursting off one page and onto the next. He shows an Etruscan shrew, the smallest mammal, curled up in a teaspoon to emphasize its miniscule size. He shows a flea popping out the top of the book to illustrate its impressive jumping skills. On each spread, he provides a silhouette of the animal next to a silhouette of an average human to give readers a sense of how the two compare. Finally, he uses a paper collage technique to capture the authentic texture and color of each animal. If this book doesn't have your kids shouting "Awesome!" none will.

Hondo & Fabian

Peter McCarty, Author and Illustrator

Henry Holt and Company, 2002

Hondo the dog and Fabian the cat are best friends. They live in the same house, nap together, and eat together. However, on this particular day, they go their separate ways. Hondo visits the beach with his friend Fred, while Fabian stays at home to play with the little girl of the house. *Hondo & Fabian* is living proof that children's books have the power to comfort not only with their words, but also with their pictures. McCarty's soft pencil drawings are dreamlike. The feeling of solitude they evoke is contagious. It would be difficult for anyone, young or old, to pick up this book and not be completely charmed by McCarty's characters. And the book's clear-cut organization, which juxtaposes the events of Hondo's day with the events of Fabian's, can be easily emulated by young writers.

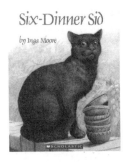

Six-Dinner Sid

Inga Moore, Author and Illustrator

Simon & Schuster Books for Young Readers, 1991

Sid is one crafty kitty. Instead of taking up residence in one home, he's managed to do it in six by moving from place to place throughout the course of the day. The advantage: multiple meals, naps, and nuzzles. Moore bring Sid's world to life with her colorful, detailed illustrations that take us into his homes, onto his street, and into the veterinarian's office. Those illustrations are treated in multiple ways (with borders, without borders, characters on white, characters in context, etc.) to create visual interest. One of Moore's techniques that is especially effective is showing six frames on single pages, depicting Sid's favorite meals, sleeping spots, places on his body to be scratched, and so forth. *Six-Dinner Sid* proves that storytelling can be accomplished as effectively through pictures as through words.

Do Not Open This Book!

Michaela Muntean, Author
Pascal Lemaitre, Illustrator
Scholastic, 2006

Despite its title, we highly recommend not only opening this book, but sharing it with your students. But be prepared: You won't find pretty pictures, poetic prose, characters and themes that linger in your mind long after you've finished. Instead you'll find a work in progress. Specifically, a jumble of words being assembled by a pig with a bad case of writer's block and a variety of tools to help him overcome it: writing guides, inspirational signs, glue, tape, nails, etc. The presence of the reader, of course, is not helping the matter. So the pig spends the first part of the book trying to convince him or her to go away. But when he realizes that's not going to happen, he begrudgingly provides a glimpse into his writing process. This pig will have your students squealing in delight during read-aloud, as will Lemaitre's over-the-top illustrations.

Never Cry Woof!

Jane Wattenberg, Author and Illustrator
Scholastic, 2005

When Aesop penned *The Boy Who Cried Wolf* back in 600 B.C., we're sure he never imagined this high-voltage, hip-hop adaptation of it would eventually come along. Instead of a shepherd boy, though, we have irresponsible Bix, a dog that's been hired by a farmer to guard a pack of "ewes, rams, and little lambs," along with his partner, the far more responsible Hunky-Dory. Wattenberg applies her trademark photo-montage technique, which put her on the map with *Henny-Penny*, an equally amusing adaptation of a children's classic. She places animals, signs, furniture, and other everyday things in electric landscapes to create a world all her own. After reading this book to students, have them apply Wattenberg's technique to their own writing, using photos from magazines. Both process and product will be deeply satisfying.

Knuffle Bunny

Mo Willems, Author and Illustrator

Hyperion Books for Children, 2004

Need mo' Mo? Here you go! *Knuffle Bunny* is the semi-autobiographical story of Trixie, a tot who is on the verge of speaking standard English *and* having a nervous breakdown because her beloved stuffed animal, Knuffle Bunny, is left behind at the laundromat. Trixie screeches every "toddlerism" in the book to get her daddy to turn around and go back—"Aggle flaggle klabble!" "Wumpy flappy?!" and the ever-popular "WAAAA!" But they don't work. What does work is her mommy's simple question upon their return home: "Where's Knuffle Bunny?" With that, Daddy, Mommy, and Trixie rush to rescue Knuffle Bunny from the spin cycle. Every child will relate to this true-to-life story, as well as Willems's technique of superimposing colorful cartoon characters over sepia-toned photographs of his hometown of Brooklyn, New York.

Alphabet Adventure

Audrey Wood, Author

Bruce Wood, Illustrator

Scholastic, 2001

Best-selling author Audrey Wood joins forces with her son Bruce to create this refreshingly different ABC book. All summer long, the lowercase letters have been working hard and are finally ready to journey to school as a full-fledged alphabet. But along the way, *i* loses her dot. She searches high and low to find it, but comes up empty. Her teammates offer replacements—*s* offers a star, *h* a heart, and *b* a bug. Just as she's about to accept "c's" bright red cherry, the dot surprises everyone by coming out of hiding, and the alphabet reassembles and continues on its way to school to help Charley, a student there. With this book, Bruce Wood does something quite original. He places ordinary magnetic letters, which can be found on refrigerators across America, into an extraordinary world of color, texture, and movement. The result is a presentation that children will find both familiar and exotic.

A Focus Lesson on Presentation

To help students develop understanding of the presentation trait and to show them possibilities for making their own ideas stand out on the page, try this lesson. In it, students read and enjoy a variety of books, focusing on how the text and illustrations look. They make note of how illustrators engage the reader through a variety of creative styles of art. Then students categorize the books into sets, picking favorites to share with the class. This attention to presentation allows students to see the impact of visual appeal on the reader, a lesson they should learn early as budding writers themselves.

Materials:

❋ 25 or more books from this bibliography or from your own library that represent a range of styles

❋ chart paper

❋ markers

❋ stars or other shapes to create the "Mrs. Smithy" award for the strongest presentation in a category

What to Do:

1. Ask students why they enjoy looking at picture books. Chances are they'll say they like the variety of styles, colors, and type treatments that illustrators use. Let them know that it's not always important to agree on what is attractive or interesting, but it *is* important to be able to talk about why they find a book attractive or interesting.

2. Tell students that when authors and illustrators apply the presentation trait, they think about how to make the book readable, understandable, and pleasing to the reader's eye.

3. Ask students to work with a partner and to look closely at the presentation style of at least ten books.

4. Ask students to tell you some of the key features of books with strong presentation: easy to read, colorful, imaginative, stand-out lettering, realistic, beautiful, bold, and so on. Create a chart with a heading for each of the categories the students come up with.

5. Ask students to categorize each picture book from their set. If, as you work, they find some that don't fit existing categories, create new ones. Write the book's title under the most appropriate heading.

6. Organize the books by category, then divide the class into small groups. Give each group a set of books and ask members to select the strongest book in each category. Tell them that, like the Caldecott award presented annually by the Association for Library Service to Children (a division of the American Library Association) to the artist of the most distinguished American picture book for children, they will be selecting books they

admire most and awarding them special honors, with award names to be selected by the groups.

7. Allow time for each group to announce their decisions. Hang the award sticker by the book to show it has been chosen above the others. Ask each group to explain the name and significance of their award.

8. Let students read the books selected by other groups and enjoy the fine presentation in each.

FOLLOW-UP ACTIVITIES:

❖ Ask students to make a book of their own, applying the style of one of their favorite picture books. Assure them that their finished copies do not need to be as polished as those of a published book, but they should try to make their books as readable and interesting as possible. Share their books with the class.

❖ Go to the library to find additional books that fit the categories you create. Expand the categories as you discover new presentation styles.

AUTHOR INDEX

Title Index